BLOODY E
HISTO

EAST END

To Grandad Hal

SAMANTHA L. BIRD

Sam Bird.

The
History
Press

To Hooch

First published in 2015

The History Press
The Mill, Brimscombe Port
Stroud, Gloucestershire, GL5 2QG
www.thehistorypress.co.uk

British Library Cataloguing in Publication Data.
A catalogue record for this book is available from the British Library.

ISBN 978 0 7509 5233 0

Typesetting and origination by The History Press
Printed in Great Britain

CONTENTS

ACKNOWLEDGEMENTS

MY THANKS GO to Stefan Dickers and all at the Bishopsgate Institute for literally pulling the archives to pieces in order to find an image or article for my research. Thanks for indulging all my weird requests and helping with all my 'I'm just looking for ...' queries. It has been a challenge but it has also been great fun. I would also like to thank all the team at The History Press for their help and support in creating this book. My thanks also go to the Tower Hamlets Local History Library and Archives for their continuing support. There are many others in the Tower Hamlets area who have supported me along the way and I hope this continues. Lastly, but most importantly, I would like to thank Hooch and Brown Owl for making this all possible. I have expanded my knowledge on this voyage of discovery and hopefully I will only dock for a while before setting off on the next adventure! As the Stepney motto says: *A magnis ad maiora* (from great things to greater)!

600 BC

EARLY HISTORY

IN THE BEGINNING, the East End would have been a dark and forbidding place. In fact the area would have been a bog. The Thames was a tributary of the Rhine less than a million years ago, and the North Sea was the Rhine basin. With Hampstead in the north on high ground and Dulwich on the south, the Thames formed lagoons and marshes that were surrounded by the forest that covered all of the land.

Living creatures, men and animals, must have crossed into England by the neck of land connecting Britain with Europe, but by the time we first learn of them the sea had broken through the Straits of Dover and Britain was an island. At this time it was a good deal colder, so there were hairy mammoths and woolly rhinoceros, boars, bears,

wolves, wild oxen, and sabre-toothed tigers. These animals roamed the forests and hunted each other, eventually becoming extinct. For man, the East End would have been suited to cultivation with farm implements fashioned by Stone Age man. It would have been a difficult and perilous time for the East Ender, but man survived.

With a lot of forest came a lot of rain, and the consequence was that the Thames had many tributaries to carry the water down from the north. Two are of note, the Lea, London's defence on the east from time immemorial, and the Wallbrook. On the left bank of the Wallbrook, on a dry hillock near Cannon Street station, the first permanent settlement was made, at about the beginning of the Christian era. The Celts who built it probably called it Llyn-dim – the lake-fort – London. It was pretty safe from invasion, as it was 50 miles from the sea, but trade could flow up and down the river by boat.

The Celtic Britons were part of the territory of the Catuvellauni, the main group of the Belgic tribes who had invaded Britain in the second century BC. By the time Julius Caesar came in 55 BC and 54 BC, the Home Counties had become the Celts'

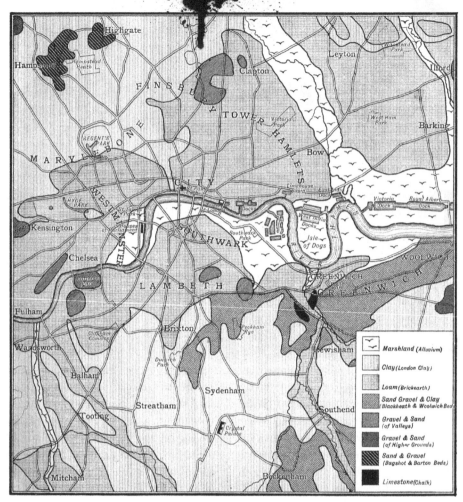

GEOLOGICAL MAP OF THE SITE OF LONDON

Geological map of early London. (Courtesy of Bishopsgate Institute)

stronghold in Britain. The Celts were fierce and undisciplined and prone to fighting amongst themselves. They were warriors who were tall, fair-skinned with red or yellow hair, and fond of bright clothes and ornament. They were energetic, musical, and idealistic. They were also daring and clever seamen who traded with the Continent. Ratcliff (the red cliff) as the Saxons were to later name it, was, for the Celts, a convenient landing place nearby. Ever since, the East End has had a close maritime link with the mother-city.

THE ROMANS

NINETY YEARS AFTER Julius Caesar called off his invasion of Britain, Emperor Claudius began the real occupation of Britain by the Romans. In AD 43 Claudius marched with his legions and his elephants down the British trackway to Old Ford and crossed the Lea to capture Colchester. Within the space of twenty years all of southern England became Rome's. Boudicca's defeat and death in AD 61 marked the end of Celtic power in the South of England and the Roman's replaced 'Albion', the Celtic name for the area, with 'Britain'. The term 'Great Britain' was not invented for

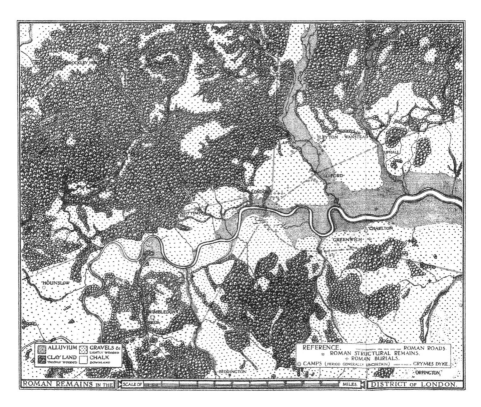

Physiographical map of the London district in Roman times. (Author's collection)

another 1,600 years, however, when James I joined the kingdoms of England and Scotland. The Romans also tried to change London's name to 'Augusta' but failed.

The Romans fortified London, which until then had been little more than a commercial port. They built their citadel on the other side of the Wallbrook and enclosed the ground from Cornhill to Thames Street and from Mincing Lane to the Wallbrook. They also built the first London Bridge. Their port was near the bridgehead and their market near the port, thus making Billingsgate the oldest London market. In the East End the Romans created orchards and gardens. Closer to the city, they buried their dead at Spitalfields and Ratcliff.

For 300 years Britain grew in wealth and importance. Roads were built. Notably the road following the line of Bethnal Green Road and Roman Road was built, joining the great port of Londinium to Colchester, the capital of Britain. Another Roman road went from the city wall along to Ratcliff, which may have been suitable as a landing place for ships. Just off the line of this road, at Shadwell, the remains were found of a Roman signal station. It is believed that the signal station would have been one of a series, designed to warn Londoners of impending enemy ships coming upriver from the sea.

When the Romans first conquered Britain they supressed the Druids, the priests of the Celts, but on the whole were tolerant of alien religions. In the fourth century, Emperor Constantine made Christianity the official religion of the Roman Empire, which appeared to challenge the Roman right to rule and had been persecuted previously under Roman law. Christianity never seems to have caught on very widely in Roman Britain. Less than 100 years after Constantine's edict the Roman legions had left Britain and Christianity was nearly obliterated by the Saxon invasions that began in AD 445. Some 300 years of Roman peace had made the Britons civilised but soft, unable to effectively defend against the fierce heathen tribes from across the North Sea.

AD 450

THE SAXONS

THE NAME STEPNEY comes from the Saxon *Stebunhithe*, meaning the landing place of Stebba or Stephen. During Saxon times most of the manor of Stepney was a rural rather than a maritime area, with marshlands in the south near the Thames and forests to the north, part of which is now Victoria Park. Considering the area's later development into

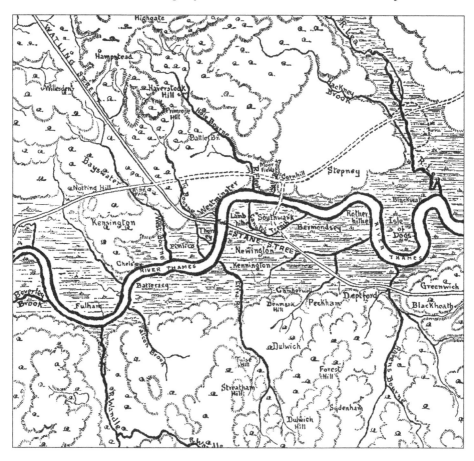

London before the houses. (Courtesy of Bishopsgate Institute)

maritime affairs, it is interesting that its original name is related to shipping.

It has been suggested that London may have been abandoned for some time, at least during the fifth century, due to Saxon invaders having little interest in urban life. Britain was divided up into kingdoms and East London became part of the kingdom of the East Saxons, which included present-day Essex, Middlesex and Hertfordshire. Later this domain was absorbed into the larger kingdom of Mercia.

The Roman roads hastened the advance of the Saxons, enabling the heathen invaders to cut deep inland with much greater speed than would have been possible otherwise. Due to the focus on roads in London, it was certain that London would be a great city. However, London is not heard of between 457, early in the Saxon invasion when the people of London fled south over the bridge, and the seventh century when it was the chief town of the East Saxons.

When St Augustine, who was sent by Pope Gregory the Great, came from Rome in the sixth century to convert King Ethelbert of Kent and the Anglo-Saxons to Christianity, he found no trace of an earlier Christianity, even though there were close connections with Christian France and Ethelbert's Queen Bertha was a Christian. King Ethelbert, deemed to be the most powerful prince in the land, was converted in a few months and in 604 he established a diocese of London. The diocese consisted of Middlesex, Essex and part of Hertfordshire. Ethelbert built St Paul's church in London for the bishop and granted much land in and about

The first arrival of the Saxons.
(Courtesy of Bishopsgate Institute)

London. The vast manor of Stepney, which covered pretty much the whole of the modern East End, from Islington to the Thames and from Aldgate to the Lea, passed into the hands of the bishop. This manor prevented the eastward spread of London, and was the principal residence of the bishops of London.

Gradually village life became centred on the church as Christianity took hold. Rather than the old rite of dedication, baptism succeeded. Marriage continued to be ratified by handclasp but was now blessed by the priest. The burial rite was altered and slowly adapted the new faith. By AD 700 the English Church consolidated in absolute communion with Rome. The Christian faith became a common denominator across the separate kingdoms but this unifying factor did not prevent wars between different princes.

For England, unity came in the ninth century with the threat of a Viking invasion. The Vikings came from what are now Denmark, Norway and Sweden. Typically they arrived suddenly in their fast-sailing longboats and killed whoever got in their way before making their escape as quickly as they had come. In 870 the Vikings raided what is now Essex and, during this raid, they destroyed Barking Abbey. They carried on to London and in a short space of time they were in control of most of eastern England. The Vikings then entered the kingdom of Wessex but were defeated by Alfred the Great at the Battle of Edington in 878. Guthrum, the Viking leader, was baptised and agreed to keep the peace. He also accepted the Treaty of Wedmore, which named the River Lea as the frontier between the Saxons to the west and the Danes to the east. As a result of the treaty, England became a rich commercial centre of trading, chiefly in wool and skins.

By 886 Alfred had occupied London and was accepted as the King of England by the other kingdoms, becoming the first king to visualise England as a whole. Alfred refortified the Roman perimeter of London and built a fleet to protect the coast as a new wave of Danish pirates came swarming up the Thames and the Lea. The Danes set up camp in Benfleet and Alfred's army marched through East London to destroy their camp and ships. However, the Danish fleet retaliated by sailing up the River Lea to Ware, where they built a fort from which they could plunder the surrounding countryside. In 896, the harvest in Stepney could not be gathered until the farmlands were protected by Alfred's forces. Unable to dislodge the Danes in battle, Alfred had the waters of the Lea diverted so that the Danes were unable to use their longboats. The Danes retreated to the Danelaw, their territory to the east of the Lea, where many of the raiders eventually settled down and inter-married with the Saxons.

During the reign of Edgar, with his adviser Dunstan, there was a period of peace. The tenth century was the great period of Saxon England, when Alfred's greatness lived on in the kings of his line, drove back the Danes and gave laws, peace and prosperity to the land. A religious revival also began in Glastonbury under Dunstan. However, after the death of Edgar in 975 the Danes attacked in force.

ST DUNSTAN AND THE DEVIL

DUNSTAN WAS BORN in AD 909, the son of Heorstan, a nobleman of Wessex, and Cynethryth, a pious woman. He studied under the Irish monks in the famous, and already ancient, abbey of Glastonbury and, while still a child, he entered the service of King Æthelstan, grandson of Alfred, and soon became a favourite of the king. Other members of court were envious of his position, however, and a plot surfaced to disgrace him. Dunstan was accused of being involved with witchcraft and black magic, and he was banished from court. As he was leaving the palace his enemies physically attacked him, beat him severely, bound him, and threw him into a cesspool. Dunstan managed to crawl out and went to his relative Æthelstan, Bishop of Winchester, who tried to persuade him to become a monk. Dunstan was doubtful about this vocation but then came an attack of swelling tumours all over his body. The ailment was so severe that it was thought to be leprosy, but was probably some form of blood poisoning caused by being beaten and thrown into the cesspool. Whatever its cause, it clarified

Dunstan's thoughts and he took holy orders in 943. Dunstan returned to the life of a hermit in St Mary's, Glastonbury, and built a small cell in which he studied, worked at his handicrafts and played the harp. It was at this time that, according to eleventh-century legend, the Devil tried to tempt Dunstan but he held the Devil by the face with hot tongs.

When Edmund, Æthelstan's brother, came to the throne in 940, he called Dunstan back to his court at Cheddar and made him a minister. Nevertheless, royal favour again fostered jealousy; he was banished once more but returned when Edmund made him Abbot of Glastonbury. Then, in 946, Edmund was assassinated and his brother Eadred succeeded the throne as king. Eadred's policy was of unification and conciliation with the Danish half of the kingdom, and the firm establishment of a royal authority. Dunstan was shown even greater favour as he became the king's guide in public policy. In 955, however, Eadred died and Eadwig, the elder son of Edmund, came to the throne as a headstrong youth devoted to the reactionary nobles. On the day of Eadwig's coronation, legend has it that

Dunstan began a feud with the soon to be king when Eadwig failed to attend a meeting of nobles. Dunstan eventually found the young monarch cavorting with a noblewoman, Ælfgifu, and her mother. Dunstan was infuriated when Eadwig refused to return with him and he eventually dragged the youth away and forced him to renounce the girl as a 'strumpet'. Realising that he had offended the king, Dunstan escaped to the sanctuary of his cloister but Eadwig, incited by Ælfgifu whom he married, followed Dunstan and plundered the monastery.

Dunstan fled to Flanders but was recalled by Edgar who became king north of the Thames while the south remained faithful to Eadwig. On his

The rood in St Dunstan's church, Stepney. (Courtesy of Bishopsgate Institute)

return, Dunstan was made Bishop of Worcester and then Bishop of London by Edgar. As Bishop of London, Dunstan was also Lord of the Manor of Stepney. It was probably at this time that Dunstan either built or rebuilt the church of All Saints, on the site of the present church. The traditional date for this is 952, as Dunstan was heavily engaged in public work of all kinds at this time of his first pre-eminence.

The structure of Dunstan's church was probably timber and may well have been something like the Saxon church that still stands at nearby Greenstead near Chipping Ongar, some 15 miles away. When Dunstan was canonised in 1029, the church was rededicated and has ever since been the church of St Dunstan and All Saints. Above the altar in the church, the rood is one of the most precious items in East London and dates from about this time.

Edgar became sole king in 959 and soon afterwards Dunstan was made Archbishop of Canterbury. Dunstan was the most influential man in the land next to the king from this time until Edgar's death in 975. It has been suggested that Dunstan might be called the first Prime Minister of England.

Dunstan was a Saxon, but his temperament is said to be far more like a Celt. He was said to be energetic, idealistic, ascetic, versatile and attractive to women. Apart from being a holy man, he was a great politician, a smith, an artist and a musician. Evidence of Dunstan the artist can be seen by his self-portrait in a manuscript from Glastonbury. When King Eadred first offered him a bishopric he was too modest to accept it. His zeal was for the education of the clergy rather than a

St Dunstan and the Devil.
(Wikimedia, George Cruikshank)

A charming legend about Dunstan concerns an encounter he had with the Devil when he was a young man:

> That deceiving one [the Devil], having taken on the deceptive form of a poor man, sought the cell of the young Dunstan at Glastonbury, peeped in at the opening in the wall which served as a window and seeing the young hermit hard at work, late on in the night, forging metal into useful things, asked him to make something for him [a shoe for his horse]. Meanwhile the Devil began to talk to Dunstan, and to mix up the names of women and evil pleasures with religion, and then again to dwell on luxurious delights, so that the young hermit soon came to understand who his visitor actually was. Then the athlete of Christ held the smith's pincers firm and heated them well in the fire that he roused for that purpose, all the while confessing and calling on his Holy Master, with tightly closed lips. When the pincers were glowing red-hot Dunstan, moved by holy rage, swiftly drew them out of the flames and seized the Satanic tempter by the nose and with all his might dragged the spectral face inside the window opening of his cell; whereupon the Devil gave a fearful yell of chagrin and vanished howling into the darkness of the night.

The story concludes:

> But from that time, more than ever, he kept himself always fully equipped for battle with the Evil One by fasting and prayer, knowing that in no other way can the fight be won.

The smith's tongs that figure in the Stepney borough coat of arms are an allusion to this great fight. It is also said that Dunstan made the Devil promise to never again enter a place where an old horseshoe hung on the lintel of the door. Hence the belief in the lucky properties of horseshoes!

St Dunstan's church, Stepney. (Courtesy of Bishopsgate Institute)

desire to enforce strictness in their lives. He loved church buildings and education, 'and thus all this English land was filled with his holy doctrine, singing before God and man like the sun and moon'.

However, in an age of loose living, Dunstan was a thorn in the flesh of the easy-going. On one occasion he even resisted the Pope, who had given permission for an unlawful marriage. Dunstan was totally absorbed in religion and it was said that, when he went to the altar, he spoke as if speaking face to face with the Lord.

After the king's death, Dunstan secured the succession of Edgar's elder son, Edward II 'the Martyr'. However, Edward's stepmother, Ælfthryth, who wished her own son Æthelred to reign, had the young king assassinated at Corfe Castle, Dorset, in March 978. Æthelred II 'the Unready', her son, then became king. At this point Dunstan's political career came to an end and he retired to Canterbury, where he died in 988.

Legends began to grow immediately after the death of Dunstan and in 1029 he was canonised with 19 May being set aside as his feast day. Prior to the Norman Conquest he was the greatest English ecclesiastic. His tomb was the most visited shrine for English pilgrims for 200 years, no doubt partly due to the peaceful and prosperous nature of Edgar's reign with Dunstan at his side. Dunstan is the patron saint of goldsmiths and blacksmiths and the date year on hallmarks run from 19 May to 18 May to match his feast day. He has twenty churches in England dedicated to him, four of which are in London – St Dunstan's, Stepney; St Dunstan's, Mayfield; St Dunstan-in-the-East; and St Dunstan-in-the-West.

AD 1078

THE BUILDING OF THE TOWER OF LONDON AND THE MAGNA CARTA

THE REIGN OF Æthelred II 'the unready' coincided with a renewal of Danish attacks on England. The chaos steadily increased until the death of Æthelred in 1016, when King Canute of Denmark became King of England as well. Canute promised the English good and strong government under the laws of their ancestors, and he kept this promise. During Canute's reign, London's trade with the Continent was bolstered and the East End is likely to have flourished.

On Christmas Day 1066, William the Conqueror was crowned King of England in Westminster Abbey. During the ceremony, his soldiers were burning the city of London. While he waited to accept the homage of the English earls, he had a temporary fort built on a strategic site inside the city walls to awe the people into submission. Later a stone tower was constructed, probably to designs by Gundulf, Bishop of Rochester, which would later become the Tower of London.

The fortress dates from 1078. At the time it was by far the largest secular building in the country and formed a

The year 1101 saw the building of Bow Bridge across the River Lea. It is said to be the first stone bridge in England. Prior to the building of the bridge, the Lea had been crossed at its lowest point, Old Ford, where the river could be forded. The Lea was tidal, so crossing it could be a dangerous task.

The Tower of London. (Courtesy of Bishopsgate Institute/London and Middlesex Archaeological Society)

square keep made out of Cæn stone that stood 90ft high. The walls were 11ft thick and it was built on a basement with walls that were 15ft wide at their base. This enormous building was to serve as a residence, treasury, prison and stronghold. There is some debate over when the keep was completed but it was sometime between the reign of William II, known as William Rufus (1087–1101), and the reign of Henry I (1101–35). In 1101, the Tower had its first prisoner, Ranulf Flambard, Bishop of Durham, who was arrested for selling benefices. His treatment at the Tower was not harsh as he had his own servants and rooms in the keep. At a feast he got his warders drunk with wine and then made his escape from an upper window in the Tower using a rope.

During Henry II's reign (1154–89), new palace buildings were added, including a kitchen, bakery and gaol. In 1189, William Longchamp, a Norman, was appointed by Richard I to be Justiciar of England and Keeper of the Tower during the king's absence. Longchamp set about fortifying the Tower and spent enormous sums doing so. A stone wall was erected around the keep; the Bell Tower and perhaps the Wardrobe Tower were built, and a new ditch was dug on the west and north sides. Longchamp also spent £100 on mangonels, a catapult for hurling large stones, when he heard that Prince John was plotting to seize the throne. The council were jealous of Longchamp's power and in 1191 they, along with John's supporters, besieged the Tower. Longchamp surrendered after three days and was exiled to France. John (nicknamed John 'Lackland') then took over the kingdom.

During the reign of John (1199–1216) there was a further strengthening of the Tower. The Bell Tower was finished and the northern ditch was deepened. In 1210, John acquired a lion and began to keep a royal menagerie there. By 1235 the royal menagerie was expanded when the Holy Roman Emperor gave Henry III three leopards, an allusion to the leopards on the Plantagenet coat of arms. It was soon after this, in 1241, that the keep was whitewashed and thereafter became known as the White Tower. Another gift was a polar bear from the King of Norway, while in 1255 the king's French cousin, Louis IX, also added to the menagerie when he presented Henry with an elephant, which the public were allowed to view.

THE BLIND BEGGAR OF BETHNAL GREEN

It is said that Henry, son of Simon de Montfort, 'father' of Parliament, adopted the disguise of a beggar after his defeat at the Battle of Evesham. The story goes that he only revealed his true identity (and his wealth) at the wedding feast of his daughter Bessy, when she was to wed the one man who was not discouraged by the knowledge that her father was a beggar. However, the real Henry de Montfort is believed to have been killed in the Battle of Evesham in 1265.

In 1215, the barons seized the Tower in an attempt to force John to accept the Magna Carta, which he did, putting his name to one of our history's most important documents. However, John broke his word and the barons retaliated by offering the throne to Prince Louis of France, who arrived in 1216 and held court for a year. The actions of the barons had plunged England into a war that became known as the First Barons' War. However, the English Church and the Pope refused to crown Louis as king and when he returned to England with reinforcements he was defeated.

With the death of King John in 1216, his 9-year-old son Henry was crowned King of England and a new charter was drafted to undermine the rebels. The Great Charter of 1216 differed from the 1215 charter in that it only had forty-two rather than sixty-one clauses.

With the end of the First Barons' War the charter was reissued. Then in 1225, with Henry reaching the age of majority, the charter was again renewed. It would be reissued once more when Edward I 'Longshanks' ascended the throne in 1272.

In 1299 Edward I was juggling war with Scotland and France and in order to obtain the money he needed he was forced to ratify the Magna Carta once again. Edward's palace at Westminster had been burnt down so he went to Stepney with his friend the Lord Mayor, Henry le Waleys, to the Great Place, just west of St Dunstan's. It was here that, after several meetings of Parliament, the Magna Carta was again confirmed by Edward I. There was also a new provision that there should be no taxation without consent of the lords, the Church and the freemen of England.

THE NAMING OF ST MARY MATFELON

ST MARY MATFELON was the original name of the chapel of ease erected in Stepney in the early part of the fourteenth century. Eventually the name passed out of use and the chapel became known as the White Chapel due to the whitewashing

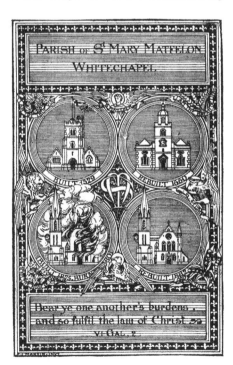

The building of St Mary Matfelon, Whitechapel. (Courtesy of Bishopsgate Institute)

of buildings during the Middle Ages to keep them clean and attractive. The White Chapel soon became a landmark on the Essex Road. The upper part of the original church tower, which stood for over 500 years, was always kept painted white and it was this building that gave the area its name of Whitechapel. The church's original name of St Mary Matfelon may well have been lost but there are a number of opinions about where the name itself came from.

The first idea is that *Matfelon* is a Hebrew word for a woman who has lately delivered or is carrying her son. It is suggested that this word was brought over by the Crusaders. Another idea is that Matfelon was the name of a knight who was a benefactor to the church. A third suggestion, however, is that the name became attached to the church on account of a murder.

Legend has it that in about 1428 a widow had a lodger in her house, a Frenchman or Breton, whom she had raised as one of her own. The lodger repaid the widow's kindness by murdering her for the sake of her money and then escaped to the parish

THE LEGEND OF THE FISH AND THE RING

The legend of the fish and the ring is the most romantic story associated with Stepney. The tale goes that a knight passed by a cottage and heard the cries of a woman in labour. As well as the usual knightly skills, he was also knowledgeable in the occult sciences and knew that if the child was born then it was destined to be his wife. Unable to abide the thought of such an ignoble alliance, the knight endeavoured to elude the decree of fate by destroying the child, but every attempt he made was thwarted. When the child had grown into a woman, the knight took her to the seaside with the intention of drowning her, but relented. Whilst they stood by the shore, he threw a ring into the sea and commanded her to never see him again, on pain of instant death, unless she could produce that ring. Time passed and the woman went on to become a fine cook. She never forgot about the knight, however, and when she discovered the ring in a codfish as she dressed it for dinner she rejoiced and went to marry her knight.

The story formed the basis of a novel entitled *Dame Rebecca Berry, Or Court Scenes in the reign of Charles II* which is linked to the monument of Dame Rebecca in St Dunstan's church. Her coat of arms includes both a fish and a ring. For some mysterious reason her monument describes her by her name during her first rather than her second marriage. In fact, despite the attraction of the legend to historians, subsequent research has never unearthed her maiden name.

of St George's, Southwark. He was apprehended in Southwark and brought back to the parish but the people were so enraged that he would pass by the church that they cast at him everything they could lay their hands on until he was done to death. It was then that the parish got the name of Matfelon. The people were said to be 'mated', meaning scared, and the murderer was a felon and thus the name was a joining of these ideas. A final suggestion is that Matfelon is to do with tolling the bell when a criminal passed the church, reminding him of his impending doom and causing him to be mated or scared. It is also said that the church was built on a field that was covered in a species of knapweed called Matfelon.

Sketch of St Mary Matfelon, Whitechapel.
(Courtesy of Bishopsgate Institute)

AD 1348

THE BLACK DEATH

THE BLACK DEATH entered England through the port of Melcombe Regis, Dorset, and rapidly spread, reaching London in the autumn of 1348. As we now know, the plague was spread by rats carrying infected fleas, which thrived in the unsanitary conditions of England's towns. Once a victim had become infected they usually died within days but there were also reports of people succumbing within hours. The plague was to rage through London during 1349, abating in the spring of 1350. Henceforth, the plague was endemic in London until the Great Plague of 1665.

The proportion of London's population to have died during the Black Death is uncertain, but it is estimated to have been between a third and half. It was commonly believed that the disease was airborne and, as a result, a number of people fled the metropolis before and during the Black Death in an effort to avoid the contagion. However, if such a course of action was impossible then the constant burning of aromatic woods or powders was believed to purify the air. Another precaution was to seal up windows with waxed cloth. The symptoms of the Black Death were inflammatory swellings, agonising thirst and high fever. There was no known cure.

There are only fragments of information on the impact of the plague in the 1340s, unlike the well-documented Great Plague of 1665. In 1349 the death toll was higher and the terror must have been overwhelming in the face of such a fearsome disease. However, from late 1348, Edward III did take general steps to ensure the continued governance of his kingdom during the crisis. In November 1348, for instance, the king closed a number of major ports.

John Corey, a cleric, procured from the Priory of Holy Trinity the land in East Smithfield. Corey had been purchasing property in the area since 1346, so had possibly intended to establish a Cistercian abbey at East Smithfield prior to the plague. The burial ground was consecrated, and thus the East Smithfield cemetery was established as a response to the crisis. It appears to have been methodically organised and managed. The implication of this being that the collection of the dead and their transportation to the cemetery was also organised. Perhaps there was an administrative body concerned with public health that functioned in London throughout the Black Death emergency. It has also been suggested that the establishment of East and West Smithfield cemeteries in 1348 meant that a decision was taken soon after the outbreak of the Black Death in London to bury the dead in specially created plague cemeteries, rather than filling local churches and churchyards. If this hypothesis is correct then the great majority of Londoners killed by the Black Death were buried at East and West Smithfield.

Stepney suffered terribly during the years of the plague in 1348–49. In December 1348 the Court Rolls recorded that four members of one family had died – mother, daughter and two sons. During the course of 1349, four more members of the same family died and their holding passed to heirs of a different name. By the Easter of 1349, the aletasters in Stratford, Aldgate Street and Halliwell Street were all dead. Throughout 1349 the Court Rolls consist of long lists of the dead. The height of plague mortality came during the summer and early autumn and no fewer than 105 holdings were vacated by deaths of tenants between February and Michaelmas 1349. The number of deaths recorded in connection with this is 121, but this is not a complete number due to the torn condition of the rolls. Due to the high mortality and heirs to land not being found, ownership of land frequently lapsed and it went back into the hands of the lords. Overall, figures suggest that more than a third of peasant cultivators of Stepney Manor were lost to the Black Death.

Death's coat of arms. (Courtesy of the University of Toronto Wenceslaus Hollar Digital Collection)

East Smithfield received innumerable bodies of the dead, a fact which came to the notice of King Edward III. It reminded him of a vow he had made when in a storm at sea while crossing the English Channel to build a monastery in the honour of God and our Lady of Grace, if he should survive the storm. In the immediate aftermath of the Black Death, Edward III fulfilled his vow by founding a monastery on the site of this burial ground in 1353, for monks of the Roman Catholic Cistercian order, and named the abbey St Mary Graces. The abbey was also known as Eastminster or simply the New Abbey. The first abbot was William of the Holy Cross, formerly Abbot of Geronden. The king gave £20 a year for the maintenance of the abbot and his monks, and in 1361 he granted £100 for work on the new church. St Mary Graces was in part a memorial or mausoleum to the dead and contemporary sources indicate an explicit connection between the foundation of the abbey and the commemoration of the Black Death.

The plague continued to snatch victims, but not to the extent of those initial few years. By 25 February 1361, the king sent a precept to the mayor describing:

> ... the killing of great beasts, from whose putrid blood running down the streets and the bowels cast into the Thames, the air in the city is very much corrupted and infected, whence abominable and most filthy stinks proceed, sickness and many other evils have happened to such as abode in the said city.

The king wanted to prevent another epidemic and to provide safety for his people. He required the consent of the council of the present Parliament to ordain that all bulls, oxen, hogs and other 'gross' creatures to be slain for the sustenance of the city should be killed as far away as possible in the town of Stratford on the east of London and the town of Knightsbridge on the west. The bowels of the creatures were to be cleansed and then brought, together with the flesh, back to the city to be sold. If any butcher went against this ordinance then he would incur a forfeit of the flesh of the

After the Dissolution, the cemetery of St Mary Graces, along with its monastic churchyard, were left relatively undisturbed until the construction of the Royal Mint on this site in the nineteenth century. The only memorial to the abbey is the place name 'Graces Alley', an obscure lane off Ensign Street and the home of Wilton's Music Hall.

creatures and the punishment of one year's imprisonment.

At about the same time a terrible plague broke out in France, which reached England and raged in a most dreadful and destructive manner. It is said that in the space of two days it swept away no less than 1,200 persons in the city of London. By the following year, 1362, the plague had abated and in May a great tournament was held in Smithfield, which brought together a great number of knights from France and other countries, with the king and queen presiding over the event.

However, there would be only a few years respite before a great plague struck once more, in 1369, sweeping away an abundance of people. This pattern of health followed by reinfection of the plague was to occur on and off until the Great Plague of 1665.

AD 1381

THE PEASANTS' REVOLT

AFTER THE BLACK Death, nearly half of the population had been decimated. The plague had spared neither high nor low, falling upon those who lived in the town, with their filthy, undrained streets, and upon the labourers in the fresh air of the fields alike. The result was a sudden and complete disorganisation of industrial life. With a scarcity of men, labourers could command high wages and tenants obtain low rents from landlords. In an effort to stop these costs from spiralling, the king and Parliament sought to make the labourers take the same wages as before the plague, and they enacted dire penalties in the Statute of Labourers in 1350. As a result, there was a gradual union of labourers and tenants of all classes against the landowners. With yet more visitations of the plague, labourers became bold in their demands and the repressive measures of Parliament and landowners brought the coming conflict still nearer.

In the midst of all this social strife came John Wikliff (or Wycliffe) and his followers, the 'poor priests'. They wore coarse, brown, woollen garments and went barefoot. These 'poor priests' won the confidence of the peasants and helped them to combine into secret unions, acting as messengers between different groups and helping to fan the flame of revolt that was kindling amongst the people. In Kent, a leading priest was John Ball. Ball advocated the equality of all men; denouncing the whole system of society based on class and social distinctions, and individual ownership of land and wealth.

The Peasants' Revolt commenced at Brentwood on 1 June 1381, as a result of the attempted collection of the hated poll tax. When the Commissioners came to Brentwood the local peasants attacked them, some were slain, and the insurrection began. Kent immediately followed Essex's example and by 6 June, Rochester Castle was taken. The next day, revolutionaries at Maidstone chose Wat Tyler, a capable and successful leader who had been in the movement for some considerable time, to take charge.

Over the following few days the revolt gathered pace and Tyler became a figurehead for the rebelling peasants. By the 10th they had moved on to Canterbury. The attentions of the insurgents were directed against the official class, the lawyers, the landlords, and anything that savoured of restrictions to public and individual rights. On 12 June, Tyler and his men were getting ever closer to London and by the 13th they had reached Blackheath.

The governing classes were seriously alarmed by the situation but the young king, showing an astonishing presence of mind, sent the insurgents a message asking what they wanted. They replied that they wanted to lay their grievances before him and the next day the king travelled down the Thames to Greenwich to meet them. The meeting proved fruitless, however, as the king's councillors, afraid for their safety, did not allow him to land.

Tyler and his men then marched on London, which was soon at their mercy. The classic abode of lawyers, The Temple, came in for severe punishment and before long the king and his councillors were shut up in the Tower. Then it was decided that the king should once again meet with the revolutionaries, but this time at Mile End, in the meadows, which was a favourite country walk of the citizens of London.

Early on 14 June 1381 at 7 a.m., the king, Richard II, left the Tower bound for Mile End, which was a village surrounded by fine meadows and used by the Londoners during their holiday festivals. Mile End was chosen as the place for a conference between the rebels and the king because it was a subtle way to get the rebel army out of London so that the city gates could be closed against them. However, that would also have meant that the king and his entire court would have been completely in the hands of the rebels.

The king's ride to Mile End to meet the dangerous mob has been quoted as an example of his bravery. It has been said that the king rode out timidly to the place of the meeting, like a lamb amongst the wolves. He was in great dread of his life, and he meekly entreated the people standing about. Clustering around the king was his entire court, including his own mother. It was a fearful ride as all along the route were dense crowds shouting their demands and giving full vent to their grievances. The intimidation and threats hurled at the nobility were so great that two of the king's escorts, the Duke of Kent and Sir Thomas Holland, the king's half-brothers, made a bolt for it over the fields of Whitechapel. The king was stopped every few yards by hands pulling at his horse's bridle.

With the king gone, no attempt was made to enter the Tower until later that day. The king had left behind 600 of his men in arms but when the Tower was finally approached it was clear that fraternisation must have taken place and, in the absence of the king and his court, the soldiers did not put up a fight.

Upon the arrival of the king at Mile End, the whole rebel army was drawn up in battle array with their two standards of St George at the fore. They fell upon their knees and said: 'Welcome to our Lord King Richard an' it pleases you; we desire no other King than you.'

After the formalities had ended, a deputation headed by Tyler marched forward and demanded the abolition of villeinage or serfdom, and the fixing of rent instead of services for land tenure. The revolutionaries also asked for a general amnesty and punishment of traitors who had oppressed the common people. They said the king should grant the petitions that they presented to him and which had already been drawn up in writing. The king, mindful of the advice of his council, granted all that had been asked. He then ordered thirty clerks to immediately draw up charters granting the petitions. In addition he also promised to give his protection to all those counties that desired it.

The king then gave the revolutionaries his banner so that they might show that they were acting on his behalf, and ordered the people to go home. The peasants were overjoyed. Nothing could have been clearer than the charters granted to them.

The main item the revolutionaries pressed for was the abolition of the Statute of Labourers. Determined to attack the statute from all angles, one of their surviving demands was that henceforth no man should serve another, unless of his own free will and for mutually agreed wages. This, to all intents and purposes, meant the annulment of the statute.

In granting all the rebels' demands, the king had, in effect, made them the legal government of the land. The king also acknowledged that he had been badly advised and led; and agreed that henceforth he would only be directed by the True Commons, in other words by the revolutionaries. This meant that Parliament was no longer to be summoned as the king was to be advised by the representatives of the people. It also meant that the income for landlords would be practically non-existent as land rent had been fixed to 4d per acre.

Furthermore, the king had given the rebels the absolute right to proceed against all those who they regarded as traitors. Foremost amongst these traitors were the Lord Chancellor of England, Simon Sudbury, and the Lord High Treasurer, Robert Hales, who was responsible for collecting the hated poll tax. Others included John Legge, a royal sergeant, and William Appleton, John of Gaunt's physician, both of whom had rendered thousands of peasants and artisans homeless and hungry. These men were accused of organising brutal bands of soldiery, who – on the pretext of collecting taxes – had roamed the countryside, raping, breaking homes and extorting money from the poor. With their new authority received from the king, the rebels were now able to execute these men for their crimes; all that they did was perfectly legal. Nothing could be done to stop the executions and soon the heads of the traitors were paraded around the streets and then set up over London Bridge for all to see.

With the fall of the Tower the rebels then went into the city centre, where many had yet to face the tribunal of revolutionary justice. The king escorted his mother to the Royal Wardrobe in Carter Lane by Ludgate Hill, which, apart from the Tower, was the strongest building in London. Richard Lyons, the great swindler, was arrested by Tyler and dragged to the block, as was Richard Imworth, the jailer of Marshalsea Prison, who was notorious for his brutal treatment of prisoners in his charge. The work to get rid of those accused as traitors proceeded at a great pace and the populace then vented its anger on foreigners. They believed that foreigners were taking trade away from them and receiving special privileges from the government. It is recorded that

Wat Tyler's rebels and the burning of St John's Monastery near Smithfield. (Courtesy of Bishopsgate Institute)

any man suspected of Flemish birth was taken and asked to say 'bread and cheese'. If they answered 'brod and case' then they would lose their head. By this time the governing class was in a parlous state.

Carter Lane remained unwatched and this oversight enabled the organisation of the Smithfield plot that was to defeat the revolution. Arranging to meet the insurgents at Smithfield, Richard II arrived with a guard of 200 men, who wore garments of peace but had armour hidden under their long gowns. Tyler, with one man attending him, rode out to meet the king, who desired to know what more his common people required. A number of requirements were set before him, calling for the abolition of the Game Laws, that there should be no law save the law of Winchester, no

outlawry, no serfdom, no Church estates, no bishoprics save one, and equality for all under the king. The king was quiet. Whilst Tyler awaited a response he called for a flagon of beer and this behaviour of drinking beer in front of the king seems to have annoyed the courtiers. A dispute ensued and Wat Tyler fell badly wounded. Tyler called out 'treason' and his followers began to move towards the court party until Richard II, with his cool head, galloped to meet them and, placing himself at their head, said that he would be their leader and fight for their cause. Whilst the king was entreating the revolutionary forces, the Lord Mayor, Walworth, was away gathering loyalist forces. On Walworth's way back to relieve the king, he sought out Wat Tyler at St Bartholomew's Hospital, dragged him out nearly dead and executed him. The insurgents, leaderless, partly gulled by the promises of a young king and partly awed by the approach of Walworth and his loyalist soldiers, finally dispersed.

The king's triumph at Smithfield on 16 June put an end to the revolt. John Ball was put on trial at St Albans for his actions and on 15 July, perhaps in grisly vengeance for the executions exacted by the rebels, he was hung, drawn and quartered. Parts of his corpse were then dipped in pitch and exhibited in populous centres of the rising. So ended the life, though not the influence, of the brave priest.

The Peasants' Revolt is generally thought to be the forerunner of the class-conscious struggle of the worker. The peasants sought freedom from serfdom, the right to move freely and choose their place of work and the right to equality before the law.

THE MURDERED PRINCES

A TRIO OF VILLAINS *gathered on the staircase to the apartment of the two young princes, Edward and Richard, as they lay sleeping peacefully in the Tower of London. Sir James Tyrell and two associates, Dighton and Forest, had been granted access by royal warrant and ascended the stairs to a large, lofty room which contained an old-fashioned but handsome bed, decorated with crimson and purple hangings, embroidered with gold and headed with a canopy ornamented with the crown and sceptre.*

Tyrell drew back the curtains that surrounded the bed and revealed the two sleeping boys, their auburn ringlets falling in curls about their snow-white shoulders. Moving carefully, so as not to wake them, Tyrell and Dighton eased the pillows out from under the boys' heads. They paused for a moment, readying themselves for the horrific deed they were about to enact. Then they pressed the pillows over the boys' faces, pushing down with their whole weight. The young princes struggled for several moments and then all was still and silent. Hesitantly pulling back the pillows, the murders unveiled the princes lying motionless, their eyes staring, their jaws distended and their facial expressions the proof of their violent and sudden end.

The corpses were carried out of the Tower through Traitor's Gate to where a boat was ready to receive them. Inside the boat was a leathern case, loaded with stones and heavy material. The princes were placed inside and the case was sealed and plunged into the river. Within a few seconds the last bubbles had burst and the waves turned to calm over the murdered princes.

The mysterious disappearance of the princes in the Tower has flummoxed historians for centuries and it is widely believed that the two young boys were secretly murdered on the orders of their uncle, Richard, Duke of Gloucester. Sir James Tyrell allegedly confessed to the deed when he was arrested for treason in 1502 but this has never been confirmed by historical evidence.

This was a period of great unrest as opposing forces sought to take the English throne. Between 1455–85 the Wars of the Roses raged as the result of social and financial troubles following

The young princes sleeping before their gruesome murder! (Courtesy of Bishopsgate Institute)

the Hundred Years' War – combined with the weak rule of Henry VI – which revived interest in the alternative claim to the throne of Richard, Duke of York, who also descended from Edward III. In 1460 Richard died but his son took command of the Yorkist forces and the following year he crowned himself Edward IV. Henry VI was imprisoned in the Tower, where he would die, possibly murdered, in 1471.

After a further period of contention for the throne, Edward IV died in 1483, leaving his young sons, Edward and Richard, in the guardianship of their uncle, Richard, Duke of Gloucester.

Gloucester was appointed Lord Protector while the princes were too young to rule but it is believed that he aspired to the crown himself and looked with jealousy upon the two young boys who stood in his path. The duke had a number of influential followers and the princes were soon declared illegitimate in light of their father, Edward IV, having allegedly been contracted to wed someone else before he scandalously married Elizabeth Woodville, a woman of great beauty but relatively lowly status. The two young princes were confined to the Tower of London and never seen again.

WAPPING'S FAMOUS SOLDIER: COLONEL THOMAS RAINSBOROUGH

IN JANUARY 1647, Colonel Thomas Rainsborough became the MP for Droitwich. He was a voice for the Roundheads, but also a Dissenter. The leaders of the Roundheads – the parliamentary supporters Oliver Cromwell and his son-in-law, Henry

Colonel Thomas Rainsborough. (With kind permission of the Thomas Fisher Rare Book Library, University of Toronto)

Within two months of Rainsborough's death Charles I stood on trial for his life. Not all of the Parliamentarians were comfortable with the idea of regicide and Sir Thomas Fairfax, the Roundhead commander-in-chief, resigned his command. Fairfax and George Monck, First Duke of Albemarle, would later organise the reinstallation of the monarchy when the Cromwellian and Puritanical movement had run its course. The Restoration prompted a resurgence of Puritan emigration to the New World with Wapping as the London embarkation dock of choice. Rainsborough's brother, William, and his two sisters, Martha and Judith, were amongst those who emigrated.

Ireton – wanted freedom from royal tyranny. However, they saw Rainsborough's support for the radical ideas of groups such as the Levellers and the Ranters as too revolutionary. The Levellers argued that the king should be elected by all the people. Their beliefs and objectives were summed up in a document called *The Agreement of the People*, which included such demands as manhood suffrage, secret ballots and annual parliaments. This was far ahead of their time and it would be another 300 years before most of these demands were met. The Ranters came to prominence after the Levellers and some of their views were similar. However, the Ranters also believed that God was in every creature and thus rejected centralised organisation.

During the Putney Debates of 1647, discussing the constitutional future of England, Rainsborough's opinions became abundantly clear. He supported the Levellers on the grounds that, having fought for the victory of Parliament, many thousands of soldiers of the New Model Army would have no representation in any subsequent election, as they did not own or rent sufficient property to qualify to register to vote. Rainsborough proposed that whoever was affected by a law should be represented in the enactment of that law. This view set him at odds not only with the Cromwellian command of the army, but the Presbyterians in Parliament and all of the king's supporters who at that time opted for abeyance rather than obstruction. His views concerned the Roundhead leaders and Sir Thomas Fairfax eventually arranged for him to be transferred away from central politics.

As a result, Rainsborough returned to the navy as vice-admiral. However, he built up a reputation as a man with Fundamentalist sympathies and in May 1648 his officers mutinied. The mutiny was associated with a general uprising by die-hard Royalists, which was masterminded by King Charles from his house arrest on the Isle of Wight. The Roundheads, aware that the upper echelons of the navy resented Rainsborough's views, removed him from his post and instead sent him to assist the Roundhead cause at the Siege of Pontefract Castle.

At Pontefract, Rainsborough once again found opposition and refused to accept the authority of Sir Henry Cholmley, the Parliamentarian commander in Yorkshire. The tension was such that he billeted his men in Doncaster, away from the main Roundhead force. By this time Rainsborough had become known as the 'Leveller General' and was heard to shout at Cromwell that 'one of us must not live'. On 30 October 1648 a party of Cavaliers abandoned their defensive position at Pontefract Castle to make an attack at Doncaster. The Cavalier force allegedly had the intention of merely kidnapping Rainsborough and using him in a prisoner exchange for Sir Marmaduke Langdale. On that fateful night they passed through Parliamentarian lines on their way to and from Doncaster without issue. They found Rainsborough's lodgings without difficulty but Rainsborough was not a man to surrender without a struggle. In the melee with his would-be captors, Rainsborough was disarmed and hacked to death.

There was bitter suspicion that Cromwell had arranged for Rainsborough to be killed and his murder caused a public outcry. His body was brought back to London and some 3,000 mourners joined a funeral parade. As a sign of respect they wore green ribbons and rosemary branches, the emblems of the Leveller movement. Whether or not Cromwell had arranged Rainsborough's death, it certainly brought peace of mind to Cromwellians, Presbyterians, Royalists, Anglicans and Catholics alike. All these groups had cause for anxiety as Rainsborough had the military ability to bring about religious and political reforms.

AD 1649

CHARLES I'S EXECUTIONER: RICHARD BRANDON

RICHARD WAS THE son of Gregory Brandon, a public executioner of London, and was raised to pursue the family calling. From boyhood, it is said that Richard delighted in witnessing the ravages of pain. Cruelty to animals was his pastime and becoming a headsman was his supreme ambition. He was notoriously immoral in his private life and once (if not twice) he lay in prison on the charge of bigamy. The family lived in Whitechapel where the young Richard assisted his father as a hangman. The mob of the metropolis' only discrimination between the father and son was to dub them 'Old' and 'Young' Gregory (despite Young Gregory actually being a Richard). Old Gregory had also achieved notoriety outside his profession as he once tried to trick his way into being officially recognised as a 'gentleman'. In 1626, he had laid a crafty trap in which the Garter King-of-Arms were conned into granting him a coat of arms after Old Gregory bribed the officials at the Heralds' College.

It is said that when he was first approached, Brandon refused the job of the king's executioner, but might have later accepted it under threat.

On the morning of 30 January 1649, Brandon was conveyed to Whitehall by a troop of soldiers. It was a bitterly cold day. The king, who had proceeded to Whitehall from St James' Palace, was dressed in a long, black, velvet jacket with a waistcoat of crimson silk, grey stockings and two heavy shirts so that he did not shiver in the cold and appear afraid. As he proceeded through

Executioner's block and axe. (Courtesy of Bishopsgate Institute)

St James' Park, the king walked between Bishop Juxon and Colonel Tomlinson, with Sir Thomas Herbert just behind them. Arriving at Whitehall, Charles I went into his chamber and continued his prayers. He refused to dine having already taken the Sacrament.

The axe used to decapitate Charles I was brought out of the Tower of London and Brandon severed the king's head from his body with a single blow. Charles' head was picked up and shown to the people before it was placed in a coffin, along with his body, covered with black velvet and conveyed to his lodgings.

The king's body was then brought out of St George's Hall. The sky was serene and clear, but it immediately began to snow. The snow fell so fast that by the time the mourners came to the black velvet pall all was white, the colour of innocence. The 'White King' went to his grave in his forty-eighth year and the twenty-second year of his reign.

In the last few days of Richard Brandon's life – while he resided in Rosemary Lane, Whitechapel – he confessed to being the hangman of his late Majesty the King of Great Britain. During this period Brandon was very sick and much troubled. When an acquaintance visited and asked if he was troubled in conscience for cutting off the king's head, Brandon replied that he was. He had taken a vow wishing God to punish him if he ever appeared on the scaffold to do the act or lift up his hand against the king.

Brandon confessed that he had been given £30 for his trouble, which was all paid to him in half crowns within an hour of the blow being given. He also took an orange stuck full of cloves and a handkerchief out of the king's pocket as soon as the king was carried off from the scaffold. He was offered 20s for the orange by a gentleman living in Whitehall, which he refused, but he later sold it for 10s in Rosemary Lane.

At about 6 p.m. on that fateful day, Brandon returned home to his wife and gave her the money, saying that it was 'the dearest money that he ever earn'd in his life'.

Brandon died in June 1649 and a great multitude of people stood waiting to see his corpse carried into Whitechapel churchyard. Some cried out that he was a rogue and should be hanged and buried in the dunghill. Others said he should be quartered for executing the king. In the end his coffin was carried into the churchyard with a bunch of rosemary at each end and on the top a rope tied across from one end to the other.

AD 1652

THE WITCH
OF WAPPING

WITH THE ON-GOING troubles of the plague, the population of the East End was decimated. People were horrified by the many deaths and thought that they were being punished by God. The general attitude towards witches and witchcraft hardened. Witches were condemned as being allied with Satan and it was believed that they deliberately set out to destroy society. In 1563 the Witchcraft Act was passed, making witchcraft a capital offence.

The Witch of Wapping was Joan Peterson. She lived in Spruce Island, near Wapping and was condemned for practicing witchcraft.

At the time there were two sorts of witches: good and bad. Peterson, however, was a mixture of both and although it was clearly proven that she had done much mischief, there were also witnesses who attested that she had cured diseases. For example, one man had been so grievously troubled with a headache that he had not taken any rest for five weeks and, having asked many doctors for a cure without success, he turned to Peterson for help. He was given a drink, which he drunk of three

times, and thereafter he proclaimed that he was as well as he had ever been. Peterson could also provide love potions or perform any number of odd bits of harmless homely magic for a small fee.

Another example of Peterson's powers for good was demonstrated when she cured a cow that was believed to be bewitched. A cow keeper's wife approached Peterson for help and promised her a reward if she could cure the cow. Peterson asked the woman to save some of the cow's urine and bring it to her, which she did. Peterson then set the pot of urine in the fire and shortly afterwards the water rose up in bubbles. Peterson then showed the cow's owner the face of the woman suspected of bewitching the cow in the bubbles and prescribed what she should do to cure the cow. The cow's owner was satisfied that the spell was broken and the cow duly recovered.

Nevertheless, some of Peterson's actions were deemed to be evil and on 7 April she appeared at the Old Bailey and was condemned to die in view of the testimonies brought against her. She was taken to court by one Christopher Wilson, who, when he was very sick and weak, had approached Peterson to ask for a cure. In a short time Peterson had indeed cured him and subsequently demanded her fee. However, Wilson refused to pay her as much as they had originally agreed and Peterson threatened him, saying, 'You had better have given me my money, for you shall be ten times worse than ever you were'. Suddenly, Wilson fell into a very strange fit. For twelve hours he raged and raved like a madman. Then, for the next twelve hours he slobbered with his tongue hanging out and walked up and down like a man possessed. Wilson remained in this condition for a few days before becoming very sick and languishing away. When he recovered sufficiently, Wilson took Peterson to court, certain that she had bewitched him.

This was not, moreover, Peterson's only offence. Other accusations were also made in court, the next account concerning Wilson's neighbours and their young child. It was reported that the child had been very strangely tormented with fits, the like of which had never been seen before, which continued over a few days and brought great grief to the parents, who believed that their child might depart this world at any moment. The parents took it in turns to watch over the child each night until one day two female neighbours offered to watch the youngster while the parents rested. At about midnight the two women caught sight of what they thought was a great black cat, which came up to the cradle side and rocked the cradle. One of the women took up the fire-fork to strike the cat but it immediately vanished. An hour later the apparition returned and this time the other woman drew back her leg in preparation to kick the animal, but again it disappeared. However, after a short space of time, the leg that had been aimed at the cat began to swell,

causing its owner considerable pain. The women were both afraid and called up the master of the house so that they could take their leave. On their way home the women met a baker, who was a neighbour's servant. He told the women that he had seen a great black cat that had frightened him so much that his hair had stood on end. The women told him about their night's events and the baker immediately declared that the cat must have been called up by a witch or was, in fact, Peterson herself in animal form.

On another occasion, Peterson's maid servant was lying, at night, with her mistress in bed and Peterson told her that a squirrel would visit during the night and that her maid should not be afraid as it would do her no harm. Accordingly, at about midnight, a squirrel, or something in its likeness, appeared and went over the maid to Peterson. The maid was so frightened that she lay as if she were in a trance. Peterson and the squirrel talked together for a great part of the night but the maid was so bewitched by what she saw, that she could not remember a word of the discourse. Also, Peterson's

---

THE CROWN JEWELS

Colonel Thomas Blood was perhaps one of the luckiest of men. In May 1671 he stole the Crown jewels from the Tower. He was captured but subsequently pardoned by Charles II, who restored to him a large grant of land that had been awarded him for his zeal in the Parliamentarian cause but then cancelled at the Restoration.

---

son, a boy of about 7 or 8 years old, was asked by some of his school friends how his mother could do such strange things. The boy replied that she had a squirrel that had taught her what she should do.

These and other strange stories being proved against her, Peterson was condemned to be hanged at Tyburn on Monday, 12 April 1652. Peterson's conviction was further ensured by the presence of Sir John Danvers, a member of Cromwell's council who had apparently been sent to ensure that a verdict of guilt was found. The reason for Danver's presence at Peterson's case only came to light after her hanging and was to cause public outcry. It was revealed that a number of gentlemen who were high in Cromwell's favour stood to inherit a fair-sized legacy but for the presence of a certain Mistress Levingstone. Levingstone was legally ahead of them in the queue for the money and the gentleman had approached Peterson, asking her to use her special powers to dispose of the troublesome lady. Peterson, however, would have none of this distasteful business, even when the men tried to bribe her with £100, a considerable amount of money in those days. Peterson's refusal was her undoing. The gentlemen felt that they could not let her go free in case she exposed them for attempted murder and therefore the case of witchcraft was brought against her. Some stories suggest that even on the day of Peterson's trial there were men standing at the entrance to the court offering money to anyone who would speak out against her. Sadly, by the time the sordid business came to light the gentlemen in question had either lost their positions or were dead.

AD 1683

THE EARL OF ESSEX: SUICIDE OR MURDER?

IN JUNE 1683, Arthur Capel, the Earl of Essex, had been arrested and charged with high treason. He was accused of conspiring to assassinate King Charles II and the Duke of York in the Rye House Plot.

On the fateful morning of 13 July 1683, Paul Bromeny, a servant of the Earl of Essex, looked for him in his rooms in the Tower of London. Essex was not in the bedchamber so Bromeny concluded that he was in the close-stool closet (the toilet). The closet door was shut but after waiting a little time Bromeny knocked at the door. There was no reply. He pushed the door open and lifted the curtain. Essex was slumped in a pool of blood with a razor beside him. His throat was slashed and his windpipe was severed; he was almost decapitated.

Moments after the discovery of his body, the coroner of the Tower had begun summoning men to serve as jurors at the inquest and rounded up witnesses. Essex's body was removed from the closet and he was washed and prepared for burial. An inquest was held the next day while Essex was laid out in another part of the Tower and twenty-three jurors were sworn in to hear the evidence. The jurors were selected from unusually prominent and prosperous householders as this was a crucial case and the government wished to include persons whose rank would lend credence to their findings.

The jury heard the testimony of his servant, the warder and the two surgeons and also examined the room in which Essex had died. Bromeny was the main witness. He testified that a couple of days before his death Essex had asked him for a penknife with which to cut his nails. The knife had been left at the country residence of Essex, however, and therefore he asked for a razor, as it would do the job just as well. Essex retired to his quarters and was never seen alive again. Bromeny confirmed that the razor found in the closet was the same one he had given Essex. The warder corroborated his story. The surgeon's testimony described the terrible wound on Essex's throat and said that it would have killed him instantly.

Although there were suspicions that murder had been committed, the evidence seemed undeniable and

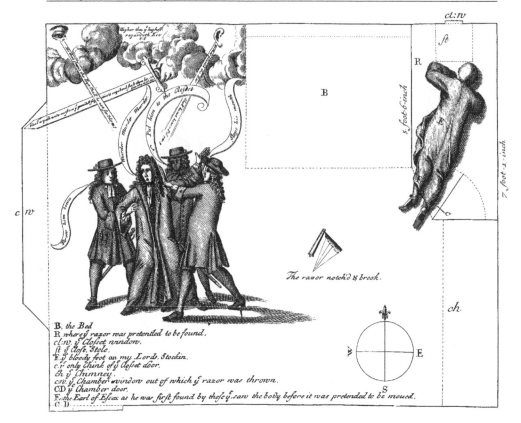

A contemporary depiction of the crime scene, suggesting that the Earl of Essex had been murdered.
This view was later discounted by the jury. (Courtesy of Bishopsgate Institute)

the jury returned a verdict of self-murder (suicide). In the jury's view, Essex had committed suicide in a rational state of mind and this was a premeditated act. This was the harshest judgement that the law allowed and meant that Essex was denied a Christian burial. In fact, custom maintained that he should be buried at a crossroads or on a highway with a wooden stake driven through his body. Suicide in Tudor and Stuart England was a terrible crime; clerics described it as a sinful act, linked with the workings of Satan, and many people considered it to be extremely cowardly. In the case of Essex, the king intervened and granted the earl's possessions to his widow, allowing for his body to be interred at his country estate, Cassiobury Park.

AD 1701

PIRATE AND PRIVATEER: WILLIAM KIDD

WILLIAM KIDD WAS the most notorious mariner to be hanged in 1701 at Execution Dock. He was a privateer and pirate whose exploits on the high seas have become legendary. Kidd sprang to fame largely due to the sensational circumstances of his questioning before the English Parliament and the ensuing trial.

Kidd was born in Dundee, Scotland, in January 1645 but was to later settle in the new colony of New York. By 1689 Kidd was a member of a French-English pirate crew that sailed in the Caribbean, but Kidd and other members of the crew mutinied. They ousted the captain off the ship and then sailed to the British colony of Nevis. There the ship was renamed *Blessed William*, Kidd became captain and his ship was to defend Nevis from the French, with whom the English were at war. Christopher Codrington, the governor of the island of Nevis, did not want to pay the sailors for their defensive services, so he told them that they could take their pay from the French. Kidd and his crew did just this and, attacking the French island of Marie-Galante, they destroyed the

Pirates on the high seas. (THP)

only town and looted the area, earning them something in the region of £2,000. Another of Kidd's successes in the Caribbean came during the War of the Grand Alliance when Kidd and his crew captured an enemy privateer and were given a reward of £150. Kidd then added to his fortunes when he married Sarah Bradley Cox Oort, one of the wealthiest English women in New York.

PIRATES IN CHAINS AT WAPPING

Execution Dock was the usual place for hanging pirates and sea rovers. Their execution would take place at the low water mark and they would remain there until three tides had flowed over them. It is said that pirates were hanged at Wapping as early as the reign of Henry VI. There is an account of two bargemen being hanged beyond St Katherine's for murdering three Flemings and a child in a Flemish vessel. They remained there until the water had washed them by ebbing and flowing over their bodies. In 1657, James Howell describes this area in Londinopolis, saying that from St Katherine's to Wapping there was never a house standing except for the gallows, thus showing the notoriety of the place for executions. Pirates were hung in chains and would have birds perch on their shoulders, picking at their flesh through the iron netting that enclosed their bodies.

In 1738, James Buchanon, a sailor, was condemned at the Admiralty session for the murder of Mr Smith in China, and was hanged at Execution Dock, but after a few minutes he was cut down by a gang of sailors and carried off in a boat. The sailors, who had rescued Buchanon on account of his good character, managed to revive him and escaped. A reward of £100 was immediately offered by the authorities for the man who had cut Buchanon down, £50 for any member of the gang and £200 for Buchanon himself. They also offered a pardon to any person concerned in the rescue of James Buchanon, except for whomever had cut him down. Accounts are unclear as to whether the culprits were ever apprehended.

About the middle of May 1751 an advert appeared in the daily papers advertising a reward of 10 guineas for apprehending one James Lowry, the late master of The Molly, a merchant ship which had recently arrived from Jamaica. Lowry was charged by ten of his crew with the cruel murder of Kenith Hossack, foremasterman, who, during his passage home on 24 December 1750, had his wrists tied to the main shrouds and was whipped until he expired. Lowry, in answer to the above, charged his crew with depriving him of the command of The Molly on 29 December and carrying her into Lisbon. The British consul, after looking at the evidence, reinstated Lowry in command and sent the ten accusers home as prisoners. However, other accusations were made by the crew concerning the barbarity that Lowry practised on the ship. It was said that he had broken the jawbone and one of the fingers of a William Dwight and fractured the skull of William Wham. The ten crewmen advertised for the arrest of Lowry in order to deter other masters of ships from exercising similar barbarities at sea. By 1752, Lowry was charged with the murder of Kenith Hossack by whipping him to death, and after a trial of eight hours he was found guilty.

On 25 March 1752, Captain Lowry was brought out of Newgate Prison to be executed at 9.30 a.m. It is reported that when he saw the cart he became very pale, but soon recovered. He was wearing a scarlet cloak over a morning gown with a brown wig, the colour of his eyebrows. His eyes were said to be bright and piercing and, with his fresh complexion and agreeable features, he seemed in no way suited to the cruelty of his crime. On the front of the cart was a silver oar of about 20in, which looked to be an antique. As the cart took Lowry to Execution Dock, some sailors who lined the path cried out 'Where is your Royal Oak foremast?' This is what Lowry called a sickle he used to beat his men with. They also cried that he must not shame Abraham, a seaman's phrase for when sailors were unwilling to work on the pretence of sickness, and one that was used by the captain when Hassack was almost expiring under the blows.

Hanging pirates at Execution Dock. (THP)

When Lowry arrived at Execution Dock, he was taken from the cart to the scaffold under the gallows. Lowry put on a white cap and prayed with the Ordinary for about a quarter of an hour. He gave the executioner a present of some money and his watch, and then the scaffold was struck down and Lowry was left to hang for about twenty minutes. He was then taken into a boat to be hung in chains at Blackwall. During Lowry's confinement at Newgate he never betrayed any sign of fear until the workman came to measure him for the chains from which he was to be hung; he fainted and fell upon his bed, in which situation he was measured. Lowry quickly recovered his spirits and declared that he contemplated death with the utmost tranquillity, but he could not bear the thought of being exposed as a spectacle to the public.

By December 1695, Richard Coote, Earl of Bellomont – who was now Governor of New York, Massachusetts and New Hampshire – asked Kidd to attack anyone associating themselves with pirates, along with any enemy French ships. Four-fifths of the costs of the venture were paid for by noble lords, who were among the most powerful men in England, and Kidd sold his ship *Antigua* in order to raise funds.

In order to catch pirates, Kidd had a new ship, *Adventure Galley*, which was well suited to the job. He also – rather ironically – obtained a crew of ninety experienced pirates and, on 6 September 1696, Kidd sailed to the Indian Ocean. Upon his arrival he planned to capture the pirates and their treasure and return to Massachusetts Bay or England. The pirates could then be tried, their treasure condemned and the profits divided among the investors.

Kidd set sail but quickly drew suspicion on himself and his motives when he arrived in the Red Sea and attacked the pilgrim fleet, which was en route for India, loaded with cargo and pilgrims returning from Mecca. It is likely that Kidd believed he could raid the fleet and sail away without leaving a trace. When he returned with the booty, he could then claim that it had been seized from pirate ships. However, much to Kidd's surprise, *The Sceptre*, an East India Company vessel, was sailing with the pilgrims and aggressively defended the fleet. The *Adventure Galley* was forced to retreat and news of the attack spread. Kidd then made matters worse by unsuccessfully attacking a number of merchant ships as they sailed to the west coast of India.

By now Kidd's ship, the *Adventure Galley*, was in a poor condition but, nevertheless, they sailed for the pirate base of Sainte Marie, which was just off the coast of Madagascar. By the time they arrived, Kidd and his crew had completely forgotten about their original plan. Instead of capturing the pirates on the island, Kidd now openly consorted with them. The *Adventure Galley*, which was close to sinking anyway, was purposely run aground during this period and sank in the harbour at Sainte Marie. At this point Kidd decided to return to New York and claim that they had been unable to make any arrests. He proceeded home in one of his captured vessels, the *Quedah Merchant*, a 400-ton Armenian ship that was Kidd's greatest prize. The ship was loaded with satins, muslins, gold and silver; an incredible variety of East Indian merchandise as well as extremely valuable silks. Meanwhile the Mughal government punished the East India Company for the actions of the pirates and in turn the East India Company raised a campaign in England against the pirates and in particular against Kidd. By 1698 Kidd was a marked man and orders were shortly sent by the Earl of Bellomont to seize him.

When Kidd reached the Danish island of St Thomas he discovered that he was now an outlaw and that his patrons were out of power. On his way to New York, Kidd stopped at Hispaniola where much of his cargo was sold to merchants from Curacao and he purchased a smaller ship, *San Antonio*. As he gradually sailed towards New York, Kidd continued to offload crew and cargo as and where he could and also tried to acquire intelligence about his status as an outlaw. Once he was near to New York, Bellomont and Kidd exchanged messages. Kidd tried to bribe Bellomont, but the bribe was evidently not enough for Bellomont to ignore his royal orders and he had Kidd arrested on 6 July 1699. Kidd was placed in Stone Prison and spent the majority of his time in solitary confinement. His wife, Sarah, was also imprisoned. Kidd's incarceration was extremely harsh and appears to have driven him at least temporarily insane. After a year or so Kidd was sent to England for questioning by Parliament, along with as much of his cargo and fortunes as could be mustered.

Whilst awaiting trial, Kidd was confined in the infamous Newgate Prison, and it was during this time that he was offered one last chance to escape the hangman's noose. The Liberal government, of which Bellomont was a part, had been succeeded by the Tories and party members visited Kidd in prison in an attempt to persuade him to testify that his Whig contacts in New York had been plotting against their homeland. Kidd refused to betray his former financiers and thus sealed his fate. At his trial, Kidd was shocked to learn that he was charged with the murder of his gunner, Moore. Two of Kidd's former crewmembers, Palmer and Bradinham, testified against him in

exchange for pardons. Palmer had given a deposition two years earlier in Rhode Island that contradicted his testimony but Kidd was unable to obtain evidence of this to defend himself. In light of the accusations against him, Kidd was found guilty of murder and also five counts of piracy. His trial conformed to contemporary practice in the high court of the Admiralty, which offered the defendant little protection.

On 23 May 1701, Kidd was taken to his place of execution in a horse and cart. When he ascended the scaffolding, proceedings descended into chaos. The first noose split and broke and Kidd fell to the floor. He was hastily grabbed by guards and held while a second rope was secured. This time, the rope did its job.

Following his death, the tale of Captain Kidd passed into folklore. His story was used as a cautionary tale against greed and deceit with the Newgate Calendar declaring that the story gave a lot of truth to the old saying that 'honesty is the best policy'. Many stories circulated about the wealth that Kidd had acquired on his voyages. It is said that Kidd's booty amounted to as much as £400,000. This led treasure hunters from Nova Scotia to the South China Sea to try and find Kidd's alleged hoard, all unsuccessful so far. There is doubt as to whether any such treasure existed, but perhaps it is yet to be found!

HIGHWAYMAN, THIEF AND ESCAPOLOGIST: JACK SHEPPARD

JACK SHEPPARD WAS an East End thief who was executed before he was 23 years of age. He was a mediocre thief but a genius in the gaol; for no sooner had he been confined then he would wriggle out and be free once more. Four times he was sent to the gaol and four times he made his escape. Each escape was more wonderful than the last. His contemporaries hailed him the greatest prison-breaker that had ever been seen.

Jack Sheppard was born in 1702 at White's Row, Spitalfields, and he was baptised at St Dunstan's church, Stepney. His father died when he was very young and his mother, who could not cope with Jack and the other children, persuaded him to go into the Bishopsgate Street Workhouse, where he was educated. After eighteen months he was sufficiently qualified for the carpenter trade and accordingly he was apprenticed to Owen Wood, a carpenter of Wych Street who bound him over for seven years.

Prior to the completion of his sixth year of his apprenticeship, Sheppard became acquainted with one Elizabeth

Portrait of Jack Sheppard.
(Courtesy of Bishopsgate Institute)

Lyon, who was known as Edgeworth Bess. Sheppard was enamoured with her and they lived as man and wife. This was to be the beginning of his ruin as Edgeworth Bess mixed with a number of undesirable characters and was herself a thief.

In July 1723, Sheppard was sent by his master to perform a repair for a Mr Baynes, a piece broker in White Horse Yard, from whom he stole a roll of fustian containing 24yds. This was believed to be his first theft. Shortly after this he robbed the gentleman once more, this time breaking into the property and taking £7 out of the till and further goods to the value of £17. Sheppard was apprehended and committed to Newgate where he confessed to how he committed the crime. He described how he had taken up the iron bars at the cellar windows and then, after committing the robbery, he had nailed them down again. Without an obvious break-in, Mr Baynes had, in fact, initially accused a female lodger in the house of the robbery.

Sheppard and Owen Wood parted company ten months prior to the end of his apprenticeship. Bereft of the good and careful patronage of his master, Sheppard fell into bad company and became acquainted with such wicked wretches as Joseph Blake, alias Blueskin, and Dowling James Sykes, alias Hell and Fury. He took shelter in the house of Mr Charles in Mayfair and, when he was asked to assist with some repairs, Sheppard took the opportunity to rob the people of the house, stealing £7 10s in coins, five large silver spoons, six plain forks, four teaspoons, six plain gold rings, four suits to wear and linen of a considerable value.

By now, robbery was Sheppard's way of life and London provided him with plenty of opportunities. One day, however, he met his old acquaintance James Sykes, who invited him to eat and play skittles at the Seven Dials. While they were playing, Sykes secretly sent for Mr Price, a constable in St Giles' parish, and he charged Sheppard with robbing a Mr Cook. Sheppard was sent before Justice Parry, who ordered him to St Giles' roundhouse until the next morning, for further questioning. He was confined in the upper part of the roundhouse but within two hours Sheppard had made his escape, climbing up to the roof of the building and then tying together a sheet and a blanket in order to descend to the churchyard below. Although a hue and cry was made as he scrambled down to the ground, he evaded those who sought to apprehend him.

On the evening of 19 May, Sheppard was with another robber called Benson. They were passing through Leicester Fields where a gentleman was accusing a woman of attempting to steal his watch and a crowd was gathering. Sheppard and Benson got into the thick of the crowd and decided that they would take the watch themselves, picking the gentleman's pocket. In a moment the gentleman realised what had happened and cried 'Stop thief!' Sheppard and Benson took to their heels but a sergeant of the guard at Leicester House seized Sheppard.

This time Sheppard was taken to St Ann's roundhouse. The following morning Edgeworth Bess came to visit him but she was also arrested. The couple were then taken before Justice Walker and both were charged with robbery – as Bess had been involved in a robbery at Drury Lane back in February. Justice Walker committed them both to the New Prison, Clerkenwell.

Five days later they made their escape after Sheppard was supplied with a file and gimlets by his friends. Using these tools he was able to remove an iron bar and a stout wooden beam from the window. He lowered Bess and then himself, using blankets tied together, into the courtyard some 25ft below. They were not free yet, however, and Sheppard inserted the gimlets into the gatepost and used them as a scaling ladder to climb the outside wall of the prison. When he reached the top, he pulled up Bess and then they slid down on to the street below and freedom.

Mr Kneebone, a woollen draper in the Strand, had received a caution that his home was to be broken into that very night. As such he ordered his servants to sit up waiting and had the watchman in the street observe his house. At about 2 a.m. Sheppard and his gang were at the door. They were unable to enter but a maidservant heard them say that they would return. This they did on Sunday, 12 July when Sheppard, Blueskin and a William Field arrived at about midnight. They cut two large oaken bars over the cellar window at the back of the house and entered before quickly making their way up the cellar stair, through the three bolts and a large padlock and into the shop. They stole 108yds of broad woollen cloth, 5yds of blue baize, a little tie wig, a beaver hat, two silver spoons, a handkerchief and penknife, amounting in total to around £50. However, they were not apprehended.

Then, on 20 July, Sheppard and Blueskin committed a highway robbery on John Pargiter of Hampstead and robbed him of 8s. The next day the two were even more successful when they stopped a stagecoach and relieved one of the passengers of 20s.

Sheppard's wickedness was now drawing to a close as Mr Kneebone had applied to Jonathan Wild to capture him. On 22 July, Edgeworth Bess was taken by Jonathan Wild and she told him where to find Sheppard. Justice Blackerby accordingly issued a warrant and the next day Sheppard was apprehended at the house of Blueskin's mother, in Rosemary Lane, Whitechapel. The following day Sheppard was brought before Justice Blackerby where he confirmed the robberies on the highway and at the house of Mr Kneebone and others. He was committed to Newgate and at his trial the facts were clearly proved and he was sentenced to death. Sheppard begged for transportation, but to no avail.

However, Sheppard escaped from the condemned hold at Newgate, a dismal dungeon on the ground floor, with a spike-crested door that opened into the entrance hall of the gaol. Tools were once again smuggled in for him and he was soon busy on the prison bars. Almost every day friends came to talk to him through the grill above the door. During these visits he would saw with a file at a spike. When he had finally cut through the spike, which was not until after the death warrant had arrived and the day of his execution was imminent, Bess and another woman paid him a visit after nightfall.

The turnkeys were carousing around a table that hid the entrance of the condemned hold from their view, and Sheppard took full advantage of this. He broke off the weakened spike, managed to squeeze through the narrow opening and, with the aid of Bess and the other woman, he crawled over the top of the door. Sheppard then dashed across the lodge and fled through an open gateway. His gaolers did not discover his flight until later that evening. Never before had such an audacious flaunting of justice been committed and Sheppard's name was soon on everyone's lips.

Sheppard now needed somewhere to hide and so he engaged the help of a trusted comrade, William Page, a butcher's boy, to help him to disguise himself. However, it wasn't long before the turnkeys of Newgate learnt that Sheppard's new haunt was Finchley Common. Arriving at the place in question they found Sheppard pretending to be a butcher alongside Page and recaptured him.

Sheppard's masterpiece of escapology occurred on 15 October 1724. The turnkeys had locked him up in one of the strongest cells on the third floor in the centre of the gaol. Sheppard

Jack Sheppard in his prison cell.
(Courtesy of Bishopsgate Institute)

was also cuffed firmly at his hands and feet, and his ankles were fastened by a heavy pair of fetters (chains that were stapled to the floor). The turnkeys, believing that it would be impossible for him to escape, left him at 3 p.m. on 15 October and did not return until the next morning. By this time Sheppard had long since gone, having made his escape by 9 p.m.

Sheppard had managed to slip his hands through the handcuffs. He then broke the chains on his legs and finally picked the padlock that held him to the floor. Now able to move freely, Sheppard removed an iron bar from across the chimney by loosening the brickwork with a fragment of his fetters. He used the bar to make a hole in the ceiling through which he ascended to the room above. However, this new cell presented a problem when he realised that the door that had not been opened for several years. Eventually Sheppard managed to wrench off the lock and, proceeding through another door at the end of the corridor, he made his way into the chapel. Once in the chapel the two gates of spike-crested grill enclosing the convicts' pews only took a few moments for him to break, but the last two doors proved the greatest difficulty: for the first door he had to wrench the lock box off and for the second he was forced to remove the middle of the main post in order to break through it. Freedom was nearly within his grasp. Sheppard then returned to his cell to fetch his blankets and lowered himself from the top of the prison on to the roof of an adjoining house from which he descended once more to freedom.

The execution of Jack Sheppard. (Courtesy of Bishopsgate Institute)

The nation was in awe of Sheppard's achievement. When he was recaptured a fortnight later, men of rank and fashion flocked to Newgate to see him. On 10 November, Sheppard was brought before the Court of the King's Bench, Westminster, where the sentence of death was pronounced against him by Justice Powys. He was then taken from Middle Stone room and put into the condemned hold. Sheppard never gave up hope of making yet another grand escape. A visitor had given him a penknife, which he kept in his pocket, and he planned to lean forward in the cart taking him to the gallows and cut the cord that tied his hands. Then, as the cart neared Little Turnstile, he would throw himself amongst the crowd and make his escape amongst the mob. However, the scheme was discovered when an officer examined Sheppard's pockets and cut himself on the penknife. Sheppard, the ever positive, hatched yet another plan. He urged some of his acquaintances that as soon as possible, after his body had been cut down, they should place him in a warm bed and let him bleed. He believed that such care might bring him back to life.

On Monday, 16 November 1724, Sheppard, aged 23, was executed at Tyburn. He died with great difficulty and was much pitied by the mob. After about a quarter of an hour, he was cut down by a soldier and delivered to his friends who carried him to Barley Mow in Long Acre. They may have put him in a warm bed to let him bleed but it did not revive him for that evening Sheppard was buried at St Martin's-in-the-Field churchyard – his luck had run out!

YOUNG AMAZON SNELL: HANNAH SNELL

HANNAH SNELL WAS born on 23 April 1723 in Worcester. She was one of nine children born to Samuel Snell, a hosier, and his wife Mary. Her grandfather was a military man who served under William III and Queen Anne, where his career was ended at the Battle of Malplaquet. Military service was evidently in her blood and Hannah played soldiers as a child with her friends and was nicknamed 'Young Amazon Snell'.

Portrait of Hannah Snell. (THP)

In 1740, after the loss of her father and mother, Hannah left Worcester to live with her sister and brother-in-law, James Gray, a carpenter, in Ship Street, Wapping. Soon after her arrival in the metropolis, Hannah became acquainted with a Dutch seaman, James Summs, who she married on 6 June 1744 at Fleet church. After their marriage, however, Summs stole Hannah's possessions and kept company with 'women of the basest character'. He squandered Hannah's money and deserted her, pregnant and facing a life in poverty. Hannah had a daughter Susanna, who was born in September 1746 but only lived a few months, dying in January 1747.

With the death of her child and desertion of her husband, Hannah had no ties. She decided to transform herself into a man and used a suit of her brother-in-law's clothes for this purpose. There are two possible reasons for this; firstly to find her errant husband or secondly to escape the poverty she was living in, in Wapping. Hannah even took the name of her brother-in-law, James Gray. She travelled to Coventry and, on 27 November 1747, she enlisted in General Guise's regiment, in the company belonging to Captain Miller. With the North being the seat of war, and her regiment being at Carlisle, Hannah and seventeen other recruits left Coventry to join the regiment after a march of three weeks, an undertaking she performed with as much ease as any one of her comrades.

Once in Carlisle, Hannah was instructed in military exercises, and was soon able to perform them with great skill and dexterity. All was going well until Hannah's sergeant, Davis, developed a passion for a young woman in town and sought Hannah's assistance in bringing his ignoble designs to fruition. Hannah, pretending to help, secretly disclosed the whole affair to the intended victim and warned her of the danger that she faced. In doing this, Hannah gained the confidence of the young woman, which enraged the jealous Davis. It wasn't long before Davis sought his revenge and seized an opportunity to charge his supposed rival with neglect of duty, for which Hannah was sentenced to receive 600 lashes. It is said that 500 were inflicted but the remaining 100 were remitted due to the intercession of some of the officers. However, the resentment of the jealous Davis still persisted and he relished any opportunity to mortify Hannah; giving her duties that he knew would be difficult or disagreeable.

Shortly after this occurrence, there was another cause for unease. A fresh recruit, a native from Worcester who had lodged in the house of Hannah's brother-in-law, joined her regiment and she was apprehensive of being discovered. She was so worried that she resolved to desert and, gathering together as much money as she could, she set off on foot for Portsmouth. About a mile from Carlisle, Hannah saw a group of people picking peas. Their clothes were lying some distance from them so she exchanged her regimental jacket for one of their old coats and proceeded on her journey.

When Hannah arrived in Liverpool, she stopped at a small public house, where she acted the gallant and rendered the innkeeper jealous of his wife. The innkeeper attempted to attack Hannah but was overcome and the following day Hannah left for Chester. At Chester, Hannah took lodgings in a private house where a young mantua (a coat-like female garment) maker resided and with whom Hannah contrived to ingratiate herself. Hannah pushed her suit with much ardour, till on some pretence she obtained 5 guineas from the unsuspecting female. Leaving Chester, Hannah next engaged with a widow at Winchester but here she was not quite so successful. Hannah had met her match; the widow emptied her pockets, leaving her to ruminate on her folly and finish her journey on foot with only a few shillings.

It took Hannah about a month to travel from Carlisle to Portsmouth where she soon enlisted as a marine in Colonel Fraser's regiment, which was part of Admiral Edward Boscawen's forces in the war against France. Hannah's disguise went unnoticed by John Rozier, the captain of the *Swallow*, and she set sail with them for the East Indies.

Hannah's skills in washing, mending and cooking for her messmates were soon remarked upon and these good offices obtained her the notice of

Mr Wyegate, one of the lieutenants of the marines, who requested her to become one of their mess. This offer Hannah readily accepted, and she soon became a great favourite with the crew.

A short time later the *Swallow* sustained considerable damage in a storm and was obliged to put into the port of Lisbon to refit. After a month of repairs, they set sail to rejoin the fleet, but the night after departure another storm destroyed the greater part of the rigging, reducing her to little more than a wreck.

The ship was repaired for a second time at Gibraltar and then made her way to the Cape of Good Hope to join the rest of the squadron. Here the marines were disembarked and joined the English army, where they laid siege to Areacopong until it surrendered ten days later. The army next proceeded to attack Pondicherry but, after eleven weeks and great hardship, the rainy season caused them to abandon the siege. Our heroine was at the forefront throughout, fording the river under incessant fire and remaining on picket guard for seven nights consecutively.

The peak of Hannah's military career came when there was a British raid to seize the French-held port of Devakottai in 1748. During this raid Hannah fired thirty-seven rounds and, according to her account of the attack, received six shots to her right leg, five shots to her left leg and one dangerous wound in her groin. This last injury caused Hannah great unease, as she feared it might lead to the discovery of her sex. As a result, she concealed her wound from the surgeons, only entrusting the secret to a black woman who attended her, and who had access to the surgeon's medicines, procuring lint, salve and other necessaries. Hannah extracted the ball herself, with her finger and thumb, and went on to make a full recovery.

Hannah then sailed with the *Tartar* before transferring to the *Eltham*, which travelled to Bombay. By the time she reached Bombay the vessel had sprung a leak and was in need of repairs that were to last five weeks. The time did not pass entirely peacefully and Hannah was falsely accused of stealing a shirt belonging to one of her comrades. Although no proof was found, the lieutenant ordered her to be put in irons. For five days Hannah remained locked up and then she was ordered to the gangway where she received twelve lashes. The shirt was eventually found amongst the belongings of the man who complained it had been stolen.

From Bombay, the *Eltham* returned to Fort St David and, on 19 November 1749, it set sail, along with the rest of the fleet, for the Cape of Good Hope. The day after their departure, Hannah's master, Lieutenant Richard Wagget, died. Hannah's service was transferred to the second lieutenant, Mr Kite, and then to Mr Wallis, the third lieutenant.

It was about this time that the rest of the crew began to tease Hannah for her lack of facial hair, renaming her Miss Molly Gray. Now there was an even greater need for Hannah to keep her disguise, so she endeavoured to pass for as good a man as any on board. When the ship arrived at Lisbon, she joined the crew in every party of pleasure onshore, and she was foremost in promoting every species of joviality.

STEPNEY AMAZON: PHOEBE HESSEL 1713–1821

Phoebe Hessel was born in Stepney in 1713 and little is known of her childhood. One account suggests that she accompanied her father to Flanders after her mother died, learned to play the fife and enlisted into the regiment. The more popular story is that aged 15 she fell in love with a private soldier, Samuel Golding, who belonged to a regiment that was known by its nickname of Kirk's Lambs. When Golding's regiment was ordered to the West Indies, Hessel could not bear to be parted from him and, determined to follow her lover, she disguised herself as a man. Hessel formally enlisted as a private soldier in the Fifth Regiment, now the 'Fighting Fifth', commanded at the time by General Pearce.

For five years there were no problems. Then Hessel's regiment was ordered to Gibraltar where she narrowly escaped action at Montserrat. The year 1745 saw Hessel fighting with forces under the command of the Duke of Cumberland in the Battle of Fontenoy and it was during this conflict that she received a bayonet wound to the arm. Golding was also wounded while in Gibraltar and he was sent home to Plymouth. Still unwilling to be parted from her lover, Hessel divulged her secret to the general's wife, who she had been waiting on. Upon revealing her true identity, she was also sent home to England and sought out Golding in hospital to nurse him. Once Golding had been discharged from hospital the pair married and lived happily for the next twenty years. When Golding died, Hessel married again. It was at this point that she gained the name 'Hessel' (her maiden name was Smith), marrying William Hessel.

Hessel had many children during this second marriage – and her eldest son would serve in the navy under Admiral Norris – but once again she was left a widow. She saw out her later years in Brighton and it was here that she met George IV, when he was Prince Regent, who was interested in her story. The Prince Regent requested to know the amount of money required to make Hessel's remaining days comfortable and she replied that 'half a guinea a week will make me as happy as a princess'. The Prince Regent provided the amount until her death on 12 December 1821, when she was recorded to have reached the ripe old age of 108.

She acted her part so naturally that her success far exceeded her expectation – the name of 'Miss Molly' was buried in oblivion and 'Hearty Jimmy' was substituted in its place.

Leaving Lisbon, Hannah arrived safely at Spithead and then proceeded to London and to her sister's house where she was immediately recognised and given a hearty welcome. Hannah's story became known and she acquired a considerable degree of popularity. She was to appear in the Goldman's Field Theatre in the character of Bill Bobtay, a sailor, and likewise represented Firelock, a military character.

Hannah found that she preferred male attire and continued to wear it for the remainder of her life. She was granted a government pension and set up a public house in the neighbourhood of Wapping called The Female Warrior. On the sign was painted a portrait of her in regimental dress on one side and a marine uniform on the other, with the inscription 'The Widow in Masquerade'.

AD 1754–1817

WILLIAM BLIGH: MUTINY ON THE *BOUNTY*

IN MARCH 1776, Captain James Cook chose the still quite junior officer William Bligh as master of the *Resolution* for Cook's third voyage of exploration to the Pacific Ocean. For the next three years Bligh oversaw the working of the ship. He also assisted in the navigation and charting of this immense voyage, which explored the islands and coastlines of the northern Pacific Ocean. This was the final adventure for Cook, who was killed at Kealakekua Bay, Hawaii, in February 1779.

Bligh then served on a number of line-of-battle ships in the North Sea.

A 1799 map of London depicting Broad Street.
(*Courtesy of Tower Hamlets Local History Library and Archives*)

However, with the end of the American War of Independence, Bligh was put on half pay in 1783. As a result he took command of a number of merchant ships that belonged to his wife's uncle – Duncan Campbell, the overseer of the convict hulk in the Thames – and undertook a series of trading voyages to the West Indies.

During this period Bligh and his family moved to Wapping, living in Broad Street, which in the eighteenth century was a new wide street that led out to the older, narrower Anchor and Hope Alley.

Bligh was given command of *Britannia*, another of Campbell's merchant ships, and was approached by Fletcher Christian for a place on the ship. Christian had been a midshipman in the Royal Navy and was also ashore due to the outbreak of peace. To begin with Bligh turned Christian down as he had his compliment of officers, but Christian persisted, saying he would be a foremast-man until a vacancy among the officers became available. Eventually Bligh agreed and although the first mate, Edward Lamb, disliked Christian, feeling that he went about his duties with an unacceptable air of indifference, Bligh and Christian became friends.

In mid-1787, Bligh received the command of the *Bounty*. The vessel was being fitted to transport breadfruit and other plants from the islands of the central Pacific Ocean and South-East Asia to the West Indies. By December 1787 the *Bounty* set sail and at the end of

A SHARK IN THE RIVER THAMES

Fishing has a strong association with the East End and a bizarre incident is recounted in the Annual Register of 1 January 1787. In it there is the story of some fishermen who were fishing off Poplar and who, with much difficulty, drew into their boat a shark. The shark was alive and apparently very sick. When it was taken ashore and cut open its stomach contents were found to include a silver watch, a metal chain and a Cornelian seal with some fragments of gold lace, all of which supposedly belonged to somebody who had recently fallen overboard and drowned. Apparently the rest of the poor person's body had been digested and these articles were all that remained. On the watch was the name of Henry Warson, London, and the number 1369. These particulars were published and Henry Warson came forward, revealing that he had sold the watch to a Mr Ephraim Thompson of Whitechapel, as a present to his son. The son was setting off on his first voyage on board the ship *Polly*, which was bound abroad. About 3 leagues off Falmouth, there was an abrupt heel of the vessel during a sudden, sharp increase in the wind speed, and the young Thompson fell overboard and was seen no more.

THE LEGEND OF THE WIDOW'S BUNS AT BOW

The legend goes that an old widow's only son left to be a sailor, possibly during the Napoleonic Wars. The son wrote to her, explaining that he would be returning home at Easter and could she have a nice hot cross bun waiting for him. The old widow baked a hot cross bun for his homecoming but sadly the son drowned at sea and never returned. However, the widow refused to give up hope and continued to bake a fresh hot cross bun on Good Friday. The widow preserved the buns and after her death a huge collection of hot cross buns were discovered hanging in a net from the ceiling of her cottage.

In 1848 a public house was built on the site of the old widow's cottage and named The Widow's Son in her honour. The pub embraced the tradition that she had created and locally it became known as the Bun House. Each year a sailor from the Royal Navy places a new bun in the net that hangs above the bar. The ritual is seen as a sign of the bond between all those on land and sea. Behind the legend is a belief that hot cross buns baked on Good Friday will never decay.

October 1788 they reached Tahiti. Laden with more than 1,000 young breadfruit plants, Bligh set sail once more at the beginning of April 1789. In the early morning of 28 April, when the ship was off the island of Tofu (Tonga), Christian turned against Bligh and led part of the crew in a mutiny.

The rebels set Bligh and eighteen of his men adrift in the ship's 23ft-long launch. They had little food with them and only minimal navigational tools. Incredibly, Bligh and his men managed to reach Kupang in Timor two months later. During their 3,500-mile voyage they only lost one man.

The mutineers spent the next nine months ranging the central Pacific in search of a haven. Some of the crew decided to remain at Tahiti, where they were subsequently arrested by Captain Edward Edwards and court martialled. The rest went with Christian to a bloody fate on Pitcairn – only one man survived (John Adams), the others either killing each other or being killed by their Polynesian companions.

The causes and motives for the mutiny are much debated. Bligh suggested that the rebels listened to Tahiti's siren song. Christian's supporters argued that it was Bligh's harsh treatment that had driven Christian to it.

This was not the end of Bligh's troubles, however. In fact, in May 1797 he suffered yet another mutiny aboard the *Nore*. In 1804, meanwhile, he experienced a case of serious insubordination by Lieutenant John Frazier on the *Warrior*. Frazier later brought a case against Bligh, accusing him of grossly insulting and mistreating him.

AD 1811

CALAMITY AND DEATH: THE RATCLIFFE HIGHWAY MURDERS

AT MIDNIGHT ON Saturday, 7 December 1811, Mr Marr, owner of a linen draper and hosier's shop at No. 29 Ratcliffe Highway, sent out Margaret Jewell, his female servant, to buy some oysters for supper while he shut up the shop. The area was dangerous and rundown with seedy businesses, dark alleys and dilapidated tenements.

Jewell was only away for fifteen minutes. Upon her return, she rang the doorbell repeatedly but to no avail. Alarmed by the lack of response, she went to the adjoining neighbour, John Murray, who owned a pawnbroker's shop. Obtaining access through the back door, Murray beheld a spectacle that petrified him with horror. Lying near the window was Timothy Marr, dead with a broken skull. His wife, Celia, who had apparently come up from below the shop floor upon hearing the scuffle, lay lifeless at the top of the stairs. The shop boy, James Gowan, who had perhaps made more of a resistance, had also been killed and the counter, which extended the whole length of the warehouse, was bespattered

with his blood and brains from one end to the other. Even the Marr's 14-week-old baby, Timothy, an innocent in his cradle, had not escaped the villains. The baby was discovered with his throat cut from ear to ear.

The River Thames Police were summoned. Charles Horton, the first officer on the scene, noted with some surprise that the murders must have been committed in near silence, as no noise was heard by the neighbours. The watchman, George Olney, had been on his beat at a little after midnight and, seeing that some of the Marr's window shutters were not fastened, had called to those inside, who answered, 'We know it'. In all likelihood it was the murderers who answered the nightwatchman and it was believed that the return of Jewell caused them to leave without taking any property with them. Certainly the money was still in the till and £152 was found in a drawer in the bedroom. The murder weapon, a heavy, long-handled shipwright's hammer or maul, was found covered in blood leaning against a chair.

The horrific nature of these murders caused a national sensation. Throngs of spectators, curious to see the place where the murders had been committed and the bodies themselves, flocked to Ratcliffe Highway and rendered it almost impassable. The bodies of the deceased were laid out on beds in the house with their wounds yet to be sutured and their eyes still open. On Tuesday, 10 December, at about 2 p.m., Mr Unwin arrived at The Jolly Sailor public house to preside over the inquest. A surgeon, Mr Salter, swore that the violence seen on each of the bodies was sufficient to cause their death. Jewell, the female servant, fainted and could not be brought round, so did not testify. Murray and

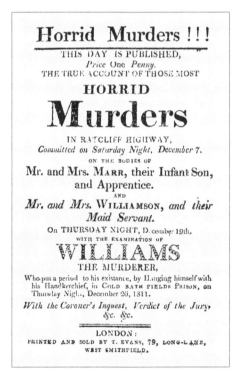

A true account of those most horrid murders! (Courtesy of Bishopsgate Institute)

Olney testified to the scene that they had found on the night in question. Little other evidence was found and, unable to trace the murderers, a verdict of wilful murder was found against some persons unknown. The terrible slaughter of this hardworking family was particularly shocking to the public as there seemed to be little motive for the crime – the Marrs appeared to be entirely random victims.

On Thursday, 19 December a second set of murders occurred at The King's Arms, No. 81 New Gravel Lane (now Garnet Street). Once again it was an attack on the entire household. The victims were publican John Williamson, his wife, Elizabeth, and their servant, Bridget Anna Harrington. Earlier on the night of the murders, Williamson told a parish constable that he had seen a man wearing a brown jacket lurking around their private quarters, listening at the door. Not long after this, the constable heard a cry of 'Murder!' A crowd gathered outside The King's Arms as a nearly naked man, John Turner, a lodger and journeyman, descended from the upper floor using a rope of knotted sheets.

The tavern doors were forced open by the crowds. The first thing they saw was the body of John Williamson lying face up on the steps leading into the taproom. Williamson's head had been beaten and his throat and hands had been cut. An iron crowbar was found lying by his side. The crowbar had no doubt been used to beat him, but a sharp implement had been used to cut his throat and nearly hack his hands off. The crowd went through to the parlour where his wife, Elizabeth, and servant, Bridget,

THE BURIAL OF JOHN WILLIAMS

Traditionally, a murderer who committed suicide while awaiting execution was buried at the nearest crossroads to the scene of their crime, with a wooden stake driven through their heart. It was believed that the stake would prevent their spirit from returning to earth to plague the living and that, even if they broke free of the stake, they would be eternally confused by the crossroads. Richard Ryder, the Home Secretary at the time, personally sanctioned this custom and for a procession to display the body publicly prior to the burial.

On the morning of 31 December 1811, the body of John Williams was attached to a specially rigged cart. The cart had a raked platform, which allowed maximum exposure to the gathered crowds, and it displayed the maul and chisel on either side of Williams' head. At the back of his neck was the sharpened stake ready for use in the burial ritual. Also on display above his head was the iron bar used to kill Mr Williamson. The cart travelled along the Ratcliffe Highway and past the Marrs' drapery shop. Outside the draper's shop, Williams' head lurched unexpectedly to one side and the cart halted. It was commented that it was as if Williams was taking one last look at the scene of his crime. Someone climbed up on to the cart and straightened William's head and the procession continued on its way around Wapping and past The Pear Tree and The King's Arms. A large crowd turned out to witness the parade; it is estimated that 10,000 people lined the streets. The Home Secretary feared that the crowd might seize the body and exact its own vengeance on it; however, the entire proceedings continued in a macabre silence.

The nearest crossroads to the murders was the junction of Cannon Street Road and Cable Street, outside The Crown & Dolphin. At the crossroads, a grave 4ft deep, 3ft long and 2ft wide had been dug. The hole was deliberately too small. John Williams' body was tumbled into the hole and one of the escorts drove the stake through his heart. As the stake was driven through his heart, the crowd's silence broke into shouts and cheers. Quick lime was thrown on top of Williams' body and the hole was hastily filled.

were found. Their skulls had been smashed and again their throats had been cut, with Elizabeth's neck severed to the bone. Bridget's feet were beneath the grate, as if she had been preparing the fire for the next morning. The crowd then stormed through the inn, in search of the perpetrators. They found Catherine Stillwell, the Williamsons 14-year-old granddaughter, tucked up in her bed, alive and untouched. The girl had slept through the entire attack, once again proving just how quiet the murderers had been.

London Bridge was sealed off and volunteers were called out with fire bells. Turner, the lodger, claimed that he had shouted for help, scaring the killer away. He also claimed that he saw a tall man in a dark flushing coat (a loose-fitting hooded coat) by Elizabeth's corpse. Another eyewitness had also seen a man of this description.

There were no known connections between the two families and again it appeared to be a random attack on a household. The principal suspect was a 27-year-old seaman, John Williams, who lodged at The Pear Tree public house on Cinnamon Street off Ratcliffe Highway in Old Wapping. Williams had had a grievance against Marr from when they were shipmates. On the night of the tavern murders, Williams returned to his lodgings after midnight and suspicions were aroused when Williams suddenly seemed flush with money although before the date of the murders he had complained of having no funds. Despite Williams' insistence that he was innocent he was remanded to Clerkenwell Gaol. On 24 December there was a breakthrough in the case when the maul was identified as belonging to the accused. The landlord of The Pear Tree, Mr Vermiloe, was forthcoming with this information. However, at this time Vermiloe was incarcerated in Newgate Prison for debt. A substantial reward for information leading to an arrest had been put forward and the reward would have cleared Vermiloe's debts. Next Williams' laundress was asked if she had washed any bloody clothing for him. She said that she had noticed that one of his shirts was torn and another had blood on the collar. Williams claimed that the bloodstained and torn shirts were due to a brawl after a card game.

The evidence against Williams was that he had the opportunity to take the maul; he had money after the murders, which he had not had before; he returned to his lodgings just after the killer had fled The King's Arms; and he had a bloody and torn shirt. This was all based on eyewitness statements, but they placed a great weight on the case. Williams was a condemned man but he never went to trial as he committed suicide on 28 December, hanging himself with a scarf from the iron bar in his cell. Williams' body was not discovered until just before he was due to be taken for another hearing at Shadwell magistrates. It was announced by an officer to the court that the accused was dead. Even though Williams was dead and could not defend himself the hearing continued. The court found Williams guilty of the crimes and his suicide was seen as a clear admission of his guilt.

AD 1831

RESURRECTIONISTS: BISHOP, HEAD AND MAY

RESURRECTION MEN CAME into existence in the early eighteenth century following the demand for bodies for dissection by anatomists and the scarcity of corpses that they could legally use. The idea of post-mortem dissection was seen as a great indignity and relatives of the deceased took every precaution to prevent such an occurrence. However, without dissection of the human body the study of medicine in Great Britain was being hampered. In 1752 it was ruled that the bodies of murderers executed in London and Middlesex were to be conveyed to the Hall of the Surgeons Company for dissection and the study of anatomy, and any attempt to rescue such bodies became a felony. Despite this concession, demand continued to outstrip supply and as a result, bodies were obtained for dissection by surreptitious means. Newly made graves were often a source of supply and a number of surgeons paid handsomely for corpses with no questions asked.

*Portraits of John Bishop, John Head (alias Thomas Williams), and James May.
(Courtesy of Bishopsgate Institute)*

John Bishop was the son of a carrier between London and Highgate, and on the death of his father he succeeded the business. Bishop also married his father's third wife, Sarah Bishop, in order to secure his assets. Together they lived in the family home at No. 3 Nova Scotia Gardens, which had been let to the Bishop family in June 1831 by Mrs Sarah Trueby. The cottage was one of a row of three in a piecemeal development on the borders of Bethnal Green and Shoreditch. The three cottages shared a well, which was situated in the garden of No. 3.

However, Bishop quickly tired of loading and driving carts and he sold the business. He next became acquainted with a gang of criminal informers and professional witnesses. They, in turn, put Bishop in touch with resurrectionists. He was employed to move a body from Holloway and before long bodysnatching became Bishop's regular occupation.

Bishop took to disguising himself as a journeyman carpenter and lodging at any house where an occupant lay dead. During the night he would then sneak away with the body. Bishop also claimed that the newspaper reports of resurrectionists Burke and Hare's activities in Edinburgh gave him the idea of commercial assassination; an idea which was further encouraged by Bishop gaining a new neighbour, John Head (alias Thomas Williams), at No. 2 Nova Scotia Gardens in July 1831. Head had also been a Highgate man who had fallen into a criminal life. He told Mr Trueby, the landlord, that he wanted the building for his new trade as a glass-blower. After a month or so

Head moved in with the Bishop family, which increased the squalor of No. 3 but gave the men the use of an empty house and garden. Head and Rhoda Bishop, the daughter of John Bishop Senior, married in September 1831. The newspapers noted with some bewilderment that John Bishop Junior was thus both his accomplice's father and brother-in-law!

The first crime was committed against Frances 'Fanny' Pigburn, a 35-year-old mother who earned her living as a washerwoman. Bishop and Head found Fanny and her son sitting miserably on the doorstep of Shoreditch church. The men invited Fanny to join them for a drink and later that night were seen taking the mother and child towards Nova Scotia Gardens where Fanny and her son slept on a pile of dirty clothes. In the morning, Fanny was persuaded to place her child with friends and meet the men that evening at the London Apprentice in Old Street Road at 10 p.m. The three met and had drinks before walking to Head's empty house, No. 2, whereupon Bishop gave Fanny a quarter-pint of rum mixed with half a phial of opium. Fanny downed this in three gulps and slipped peacefully into a doze. Leaving Fanny to sleep, Bishop and Head went to the pub for another drink and returned to find Fanny fully unconscious. Removing her shawl, they wrapped it over her head, tied a rope around her feet and carried her out to the garden of No. 3 where they lowered her head-first into the well.

As the cold water roused Fanny she struggled a little and the top of the water bubbled. Once the bubbles ceased and there was no more movement the murderers tied the end of the rope to one of the fence palings and left their victim upside down in the water to let the rum and opium run out of her mouth. The two men went for a walk to Shoreditch and back before pulling up the corpse and taking Fanny's body back to No. 2. When they were safely back inside they cut off her clothes and threw them into the privy, bundled up her body and stuffed it into a hat box, which they tied up. They then left the box ready for collection while they walked to Holborn to find a porter.

Michael Shields, a porter at Covent Garden who often worked with resurrectionists, went back to Nova Scotia Gardens to remove the body. Shields insisted that one of the men's wives accompanied him by carrying another hat box that was empty, as camouflage. Rhoda Head went with the men to St Thomas' Hospital where Bishop expected to sell the body to J.F. South. However, when they arrived they were met by a footman who told them that the surgeon was away and he could not accept any body until the surgeon had inspected it. They hurried then to Edward Grainger's anatomical school in Southwark where they got a sale. The porter, John Appleton, remarked at the freshness of the body and was told that it had come straight from the house where it died.

Bishop and Head's next victim was a 10-year-old boy by the name of Cunningham. The boy had been found by Head sleeping in the pig market at Smithfield. Head woke the boy and persuaded him to go back to Nova Scotia Gardens where the murderers gave him a gentle cocktail of diluted

Carlo Ferrari, 'The Italian Boy'.
(Courtesy of Bishopsgate Institute)

opiate grog in warm beer and sugar, which put him into a peaceful sleep. Bishop and Head took the boy out to the well and drowned him, once again leaving the body upside down for a while. The following day they took the boy's body to St Bartholomew's Hospital and sold him to Mr Smith for 8 guineas.

The next murder, which led to the gang's arrest, happened on 3 November. Head once again was in Smithfield looking for a victim when a drover's boy caught his eye. Head offered the boy a better job, which enticed him to return with Head to Nova Scotia Gardens. The drover played with the Bishop children until dusk, then he was given some bread and cheese followed later by a cup of rum with half a phial of opium in it. After about ten minutes the boy was drowsy, so Head and Bishop took him out to the yard and lowered him head first into the well. Within a minute or so the boy stopped thrashing and the water went still. As before the boy was left upside down in the well while the murderers walked to Shoreditch.

Upon their return, they pulled the body out of the well and removed the boy's clothes, which they buried. The body was then put into the wash house until the morning. The murderers arose, breakfasted and went out to the taproom at The Fortune of War, Giltspur Street. At The Fortune of War they saw 'Blaze-eye' Jack May, who was well known to bodysnatchers. May had previously been an apprentice to two Clare Market butchers, and then set up a go-cart taking passengers by day and then transporting bodies for bodysnatchers by night. The men had a drink together and then Bishop and Head went off to find a purchaser for the body. They first went to Windmill Street to see a Mr Tuson, as Bishop had recently promised him a subject. Tuson was angry with Bishop because he had been kept waiting so long that he had been forced to purchase a body from another bodysnatcher the day before. Unable to sell the body here, the men then went to Dean Street to see Mr Carpue. Carpue asked if the body was fresh and then offered the men 8 guineas and asked them to bring it to him straight away.

Returning to The Fortune of War, May was contemptuous of the price they had received for the body. The men agreed that if May could raise the price of the body then he could keep all he fetched above 9 guineas. They then took a cab back to Nova Scotia Gardens to get the body. Within ten minutes May had

brutally hacked out the boy's teeth with a bradawl. The boy's body was then put into a sack and carried out by Bishop and May and loaded into the waiting cab.

The cab made its way to Guy's Hospital where John Davies, the head porter, cheerfully greeted May but refused any more bodies at present. May and Bishop then went over to Webb Street to offer the body to Appleton at Grainger's anatomical school but Appleton refused it also. With night drawing in, the men agreed to leave the body at Guy's until the morning. May gave Guy's under-porter, Weeks, strict instructions that the body was his and was not to be let go unless he was with Bishop.

The cab then took the men back to The Fortune of War where they all spent the evening. The following day, Bishop and Head returned to the pub and, as they approached, Bishop noticed a large hamper behind the railings of St Bartholomew's Hospital, which he took. Shields was waiting for them and the three men went to Southwark to meet May. May had spent the morning selling the boy's teeth to Thomas Mills, a dentist in Newington Causeway, for 12s. When Mills washed the teeth he found traces of gum and membrane on the roots. From this observation, Mills concluded that the teeth had been extracted soon after death and that the body had not been buried.

May and Bishop made one last attempt to sell the body to Grainger's anatomical school but when this failed they went to King's College dissecting rooms between Lincoln's Fields and Clare Market, where May asked William Hill, the porter, whether he wanted anything. Hill asked what the men had and May replied that they had a boy who was about 14 years old and worth 12 guineas. Hill consulted Mr Partridge, the anatomy demonstrator, who said 10 guineas would be the maximum he would offer. Hill returned to the men and offered the resurrectionists 9 guineas, presumably looking to pocket the tenth guinea. Bishop agreed and said they would return within half an hour. Bishop then got Hill to tell Head that the price was 8 guineas and they agreed that Hill could pocket half a crown of the extra guinea.

Bishop and May went to Nova Scotia Gardens to collect the body and returned with Head and Shields to King's College. May, who was quite drunk, took the hamper from Shields and threw the sack that the body was in roughly on the floor. Hill was surprised by the state of the body. Where May had hastily extracted the teeth, the boy's lips were badly swollen and lacerated and blood was smeared over the boy's neck and chest. It also appeared that the boy's ribcage had been broken, which was probably the result of May's careless handling. The fact that the boy's arm was raised over his head with the fist

Bishop, May, Head and Shields take the body of Carlo Ferrari to King's College. (Courtesy of Bishopsgate Institute)

clenched immediately raised suspicions that he had never been in a coffin or received any nursing or laying-out. Hill, after remarking on the freshness of the body, went doubtfully to Mr Partridge for payment. While Hill was away, some of the students came to examine the body and thought it matched the description of a boy who was posted as missing. They reported their misgivings to Partridge and when he came to see the body himself he noted the marks of violence to the back of the neck and concluded that the boy had not died naturally. Telling the resurrectionists to wait while he got their money, Partridge went to the college office and despatched Mayhew, a porter, to summon the police. Partridge collected a £50 note and returned to the resurrectionists, regretting that they would have to wait while he sent a porter to get change. The resurrectionists objected strongly and while a solution was still being sought a body of constables from Bow Street arrived and arrested the gang.

Inspector Thomas took one look at No. 3 Nova Scotia Gardens and was convinced that everybody knew what everybody else was doing due to the cramped conditions. As such he promptly arrested Sarah Bishop and Rhoda Head and placed the children in the care of the parish. PC Higgins led the search of both premises. At May's lodgings a vice, large gimlet, the blood-stained bradawl and a pair of blood-stained corduroy breeches were found. At Nova Scotia Gardens, more resurrectionist equipment was discovered: spades, sacks and a damaged chisel, which fitted the injury on the boy's neck, were found. Higgins also noticed a patch of freshly turned earth in the garden, which proved to be the hiding place for the boy's clothes. The clothes of Frances Pigburn were found in the privy of No. 2 and in the privy of No. 3 the police found a woman's scalp with long dark hair.

Police enquiries elicited that a boy named Carlo Ferrari was missing. Various people who knew the boy came to inspect the body but were unable to positively identify him due to the body's mangled mouth and bruised face, which altered the boy's appearance substantially. All the witnesses could guarantee was the matching build, colouring and general appearance. So, the boy's body was buried, only, with a grim irony, to be exhumed some days later, when an Italian named Augustine Bruen was brought to see him. Bruen finally identified him as Carlo Ferreer or Ferrari, who Bruen had brought over to England two years earlier. Bruen, it is said, was a sort of prototype Fagin, who provided slum lodgings for lads and sent them out begging on the streets.

At the inquest of the 'Italian boy' the resurrectionists gave defences that they were to stick to throughout their trials. Shields was only a porter. May knew nothing of the provenance of the body and was only involved in helping to sell the body for commission. Head did not know anything about bodysnatching and was only accompanying Bishop to look at the building of King's College. Bishop claimed that he had obtained the body by bribing two watchmen who he refused to name as they had families to support. Three surgeons examined the body, including Mr Partridge, and they all concluded that the boy had been murdered. Two of them thought that

death had been caused by a blow to the head from a blunt instrument, while the third surgeon considered that the blow had merely stunned the boy and that his neck had been dislocated afterwards. Thomas Mills also testified that the teeth had belonged to a boy aged about 14 or 15 years.

On Friday, 2 December, Bishop, Head and May were brought before Justice Vaughan. Vaughan took three hours to sum up the day's evidence and then the jury took a mere twenty minutes to find all three men guilty. At 8.30 p.m. Justice Vaughan sentenced them to death, saying that he concurred with the verdict, which was supported by the most conclusive evidence. After execution, the bodies were to be handed over for dissection. However, May was to receive respite and was sentenced to transportation for life. Upon hearing this, May went into a fit and for some time his life was despaired of. In the end he made a partial recovery but his feeble health and ill treatment by other convicts on board the *Grampus* caused his death in 1832. Shields, who had been a porter for the gang, had no evidence offered against him in connection with the murder of the Italian boy. Shortly after the trial he attempted to get work as a porter in Covent Garden Market, but upon recognition by other workers there was a cry of 'Burker!' (meaning murderer) and Shields narrowly escaped with his life, taking refuge in the Police Office. This incident showed the public feeling towards resurrectionsts. The fact that some bodies were obtained by murder there can be no doubt.

On 5 December, the two men were brought out to be hanged before a large and excited crowd. Barriers had

THE ESCAPE OF THE BENGAL TIGER!

In 1857 a Bengal tiger escaped from Jamrach's Animal Emporium. The tiger picked up a young boy and was about to carry him away when Jamrach himself came running up and thrust his bare hands into the tiger's throat, forcing it to let go of the boy. The young boy, who had approached the tiger as he had never seen such a big cat before, successfully sued Jamrach and was awarded £300 damages. Jamrach later sold the tiger to George Wombwell and it was exhibited in his menagerie.

At the entrance to Tobacco Dock, which is a short distance from the scene of the incident, a bronze statue commemorates this event.

Jamrach tackling the tiger. (Courtesy of Bishopsgate Institute)

been erected to keep the mob back from the scaffold, where executioner William Calcraft prepared first Bishop and then Head. Bishop died instantly when the trap fell. Head struggled in his death agonies for some minutes, to the accompaniment of shouting and yelling from the crowd. Several spectators then rushed the scaffold, breaking down all the barriers and causing many injuries. Two men and a woman were trampled to death, a soldier had his arm broken, and a number of policemen were injured. About thirty more people were seriously hurt and sent to hospital. After hanging for an hour, the body of Head was taken to Bart's Hospital for dissection. Bishop's body was awarded to King's College, where Mr Partridge no doubt had the satisfaction of dissecting the man who had tried to sell him a murder victim for 12 guineas.

THE MURDER OF HARRIET LANE

HENRY WAINWRIGHT WAS, to all outward appearances, a respectable, hard-working, likeable man of the comfortable Victorian bourgeoisie. However, on 22 November 1875 the trial of Henry Wainwright and his brother Thomas Wainwright commenced. Henry was charged with the wilful murder of Harriet Louise Lane on or about 11 September 1874 and Thomas was accused of aiding and abetting him.

Henry Wainwright met Harriet Lane, a 20-year-old milliner's apprentice, in 1871. Before long Harriet became his mistress and assumed the name of Mrs Percy King. In August 1872 she had a child and the following year Henry gave her lodgings at No. 70 St Peter's Street where she lived until April 1874. During this time another child was born. Henry visited her and letters passed between them but it seems that they were not always on the best of terms and one of his letters requested that she did not write to him again.

In April 1874, Henry Wainwright moved Mrs King, their two children and a nurse to Mrs Foster's, No. 3 Sidney Square, and during this period

Miss Wilmore, who had known her previously at Waltham, used to visit Mrs King. However, Henry got into financial difficulties and in June he was declared bankrupt. He also had a wife and four children living at Tredegar Square and it is possible that there were entanglements with other women.

By this time Henry seldom visited Mrs King and gave her very little money. On the rare occasion that he did call, angry words could be heard. Doubtlessly, Henry was concerned by Mrs King's demands for money, which were possibly accompanied by threats that she would go to Mrs Wainwright if he did not fulfil her requests.

One day Mrs King returned home drunk in the company of Henry Wainwright and Edward 'Teddy' Frieke, a new acquaintance. Up to this point Mrs King's conduct had been exemplary, and she was much liked, but in consequence of this transgression she received notice to quit her lodgings by 9 September 1874. Henry and Mrs King were on bad terms by this time and he was greatly embarrassed and harassed by her demands for money, which he could not satisfy. The increased pressure to provide new accommodation meant that Henry had good reason to wish to be rid of her and he hatched a plan to this effect. Mrs King's new association with Frieke would prove useful to Henry and he resolved to convince her parents that she had gone away with someone of that name.

In the meantime, however, Henry set about arranging new accommodation and soon found an apartment in Stratford. Mrs King prepared to move out on Friday, 11 September, having asked Mrs Foster, her landlady, for two day's grace in order to gather her belongings. In the few days before the move, Henry also paid off Mrs King's debts and retrieved a number of items that she had been forced to pawn. Then, on 11 September, Henry purchased half a hundredweight of chloride of lime, which was first sent to his shop at No. 84 Whitechapel Road, and ultimately to No. 215 Whitechapel Road.

On 11 September, Miss Wilmore helped to move the children into their new lodgings in Grove, Stratford, and agreed to look after them while Mrs King temporarily stayed in Whitechapel Road. At about 4 p.m. Mrs King, having nothing but a night-dress with her, said goodbye to Miss Wilmore and bade an affectionate farewell to her children in Stratford, who she never saw again.

Mrs King said that she was going to No. 215 Whitechapel Road. That same afternoon, workmen repairing a van next door to No. 215 heard three shots, as though fired from a pistol, in rapid succession. They supposed that the shots came from the premises of Mr Pinnell, who had a single-barrel pistol that

he occasionally practised firing. Later the supposition was that these three shots had brought about the death of Mrs King. Once she was murdered, her body was stripped, her clothes were burned in the fire-grate and she was laid in a grave that had been prepared under the flooring of the warehouse at No. 215 Whitechapel Road. The body was covered with chloride of lime before it was covered with earth in the hope that the bleaching power would help to destroy the identity of the body.

By the following Tuesday, a worried Miss Wilmore asked Henry about her missing friend, as she had only taken a night dress and should have returned by now if only to collect a change of clothes. She was told that Mrs King had gone to Brighton for a change of air and, upon further questioning, said that Mrs King had money to buy new clothes and would be back soon. A few days later, having heard nothing further, Mrs Taylor (Mrs King's sister) and Miss Wilmore went together to see Henry. They were told that he had given Mrs King £15 before she left Sidney Square. Henry added that Mrs King had mentioned plans to travel to Brighton with Frieke and that he had given her £10 more because she was in need of an outfit. Henry then arranged for Miss Wilmore to receive 25s a week for keeping the children. He continued to pay the sum regularly until 12 June 1875, when his payments became irregular, probably because he had no more funds to give.

In February 1875, Thomas Wainwright took possession of the premises called the Hen and Chickens in Borough. It was not successful and in June the stock was sold off and the premises were taken into the possession of a Mr Lewis. A similar fate was met by Henry Wainwright at No. 215 Whitechapel Road when payment was not made on the premises. In July 1875 Mr Behrens took possession of the establishment and later that year the property was put on sale.

Henry, fearing that new owners might notice an offensive smell and unearth the body of Mrs King, resolved to get rid of the evidence by any means possible. On 10 September 1875, he brought a piece of American cloth and 8yds of rope while his brother, Thomas, purchased a chopper and a spade. At No. 215 Whitechapel Road the corpse of Mrs King was taken up and cut into pieces before being parcelled up in American cloth.

In the afternoon of 12 September, Henry Wainwright asked Alfred Philip Stokes, a local man, if he would carry a parcel for him, which Stokes agreed to do with pleasure. They went together to the back of No. 215 Whitechapel Road, for which Henry had a key to enter, and he sent Stokes upstairs to fetch down some parcels.

When Stokes came down empty handed, having been unable to find anything, Henry went up with him, uncovering the cloth-covered packages from under some straw. Henry also pointed out the chopper and spade to Stokes, as he wanted Stokes to sell them for him. Stokes, picking up the chopper,

Where the deed was done. (Courtesy of Bishopsgate Institute)

It's too heavy for me, sir! (Courtesy of Bishopsgate Institute)

asked what was on it because it stank. Henry replied that it was only cat or dog dirt and wiped it off with his hand, then wrapped it up in a piece of paper and laid it on the floor. Impatient to be away, Henry turned back to the parcels and beckoned Stokes to pick them up. However, upon lifting them, Stokes complained that they were too heavy and that they stank as badly as the chopper. After checking that they were not being observed, Henry took some of the load from Stokes and they headed out of the building.

After they had walked a little way, Stokes said that he would need to rest. Henry snapped 'For God's sake don't drop it, or you'll break them' and, after putting the parcels on the pavement, he went off to get a cab. Whilst Henry was absent, Stokes pulled off the American cloth. Beneath the layers of

material he discovered a human head and, proceeding further, he came upon a human hand, cut off at the wrist. Shaken by this gruesome discovery he quickly covered up the parcels as Henry returned with the cab. They loaded everything on and Henry set off alone.

Unbeknown to Henry, Stokes then followed him to Borough. He watched as Henry met Alice Day on the corner of Greenfield Street and she got in the cab with him. Alice Day was no stranger to Stokes, who had known her for three or four years as a ballet girl at the Pavillon Theatre, and had seen her with Henry in public houses and walking out with him. At this point Stokes found two policemen, constables Turner and Cox and gasped, 'Run after that man with the parcel; there is something wrong'. The men followed the cab, which was about 30yds away, and when it stopped near the Hen and Chickens they saw Henry leave the cab with one of the parcels, unlock the padlock to the building and enter.

The constables caught up with Henry as he prepared to enter the building with a second package. Pushing him inside they took the parcel and pulled up the cloth, discovering a human skull. Henry immediately offered the constables £200 if they would say nothing of what they had discovered. However, his bribe was refused and the constables drove Henry and Alice Day to the station where the remains of a female, very much decomposed, were exposed. The hair was still left, but it was clotted with blood, lime and dirt. Henry and Alice Day were taken to St Saviour's dead house where they were charged, at 8 p.m., with the possession of a human body supposed to have been murdered.

Alice Day, a 21-year-old dressmaker who lived in Queen's Court, Commercial Road, had known Henry for approximately five years, making his acquaintance when she worked as a ballet girl performing in the theatre. On 11 September it appeared that she had met Henry by chance and when he stopped the cab she had asked to ride with him as far as London Bridge. She noticed the strange smell in the cab but attributed it to the American cloth. Day's house was searched but there was no evidence that she ever knew Harriet Lane and she was released.

When Henry was charged, Stokes appeared at the trial and gave evidence, saying:

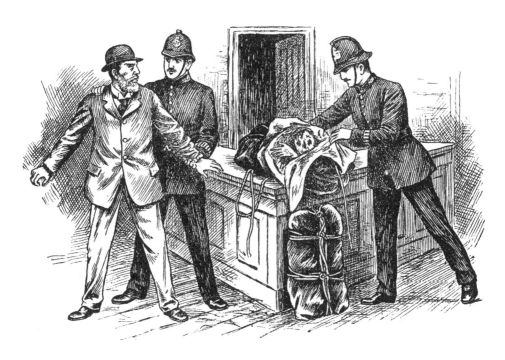

Uncovering the gruesome contents of Henry Wainwright's mysterious parcels.
(Courtesy of Bishopsgate Institute)

THE SKELETON ARMY

The Skeleton Army opposed and disrupted the Salvation Army's marches against alcohol in the late nineteenth century. Clashes between the two groups led to the deaths of several Salvationists and injuries to many others.

The first reference to such an organisation comes in August 1880 when a group calling itself 'The Unconverted Salvation Army' was founded at Whitechapel. The flag and motto for the group was 'Be just and fear not'.

By 1881 a Skeleton Army was raised in Whitechapel. They used banners with skulls and crossbones and made statements like 'Blood and Thunder' to mock the Salvation Army's war cry of 'Blood and Fire'. They also parodied the Salvation Army's three 'S's, 'Soup', 'Soap' and 'Salvation', with their three 'B's, 'Beef', 'Beer' and 'Bacca'.

In November 1882, a Skeleton Army attack was reported in the Bethnal Green Eastern Post stating that the object of the Skeleton Army was to put down the Salvationists by following them everywhere, beating a drum and burlesquing their songs to generally render the conduct of their processions and services impossible. The Skeleton Army also used flour, rotten eggs, stones and brickbats to pelt the Salvationists.

Yesterday week a gentleman I have known some time through meeting him in public houses told me he could put a pound or two my way for carrying two parcels over to Borough. I said it was a heavy price for a small job, and he told me not to ask any questions and gave me two sovereigns. I asked for three and he gave me three and brought the parcels, telling me to take them to the Hen and Chickens and that was the way I became in possession of the parcels.

Inspector Fox went with Stokes to No. 215 Whitechapel Road, where he found the spade and chopper. Fox also noticed some loose boards at the end of the warehouse and observed some loose earth underneath mixed with chloride of lime. He found hair like that in the parcels, two jet buttons, two earrings, two rings, and other articles that were identified as belonging to the deceased. He also found at least three loads of loose earth at the Hen and Chickens.

Thomas Wainwright was not taken into custody until 2 October, when he was arrested and charged with being an accessory after the act. He was also accused of presenting himself as Edward Frieke and Mrs Foster identified him as such. In their final verdict the jury agreed that Henry Wainwright was guilty of murder and Thomas Wainwright was guilty of aiding him to conceal it.

On 1 December at 8 a.m., Henry Wainwright, with fifty or so spectators in the prison yard of the Old Bailey, was taken to the scaffold and hanged.

AD 1887

THE WHITECHAPEL MYSTERY: ISRAEL LIPSKI

ISRAEL LIPSKI WAS born Israel Lobulsk. He was a convicted murderer of Polish-Jewish descent who was living in the East End of London. He was described by friends and neighbours as a mild-looking man of 22 years with an excellent character.

Israel Lipski. (THP)

Lipski started his own business making walking sticks in an attic room at the back of No. 16 Batty Street, Whitechapel. He employed two men to help him: Harry Schmuss and Henry Rosenbloom. On 28 June 1887, the morning of Lipski's first day of trading, Miriam Angel, who was six-months pregnant, was found murdered. Nitric acid had been poured down her throat. Miriam Angel, who was Jewish, had arrived from Poland a few months earlier, moving into the same tenement as Lipski but on the floor below.

On that fateful morning Lipski had risen at 6 a.m. and went to work leaving his wife in bed. By 7 a.m., Lipski had let in one of his workmen and went out himself on some errands. One of these errands, it was later discovered, included the purchase of an ounce of nitric acid from an oilman in Backchurch Lane. By 9 a.m. Lipski was back at Batty Street and asked his landlady to fetch him some coffee. The landlady duly brought the coffee, but Lipski was not in his room. The prosecution believed that at this time Lipski had entered Angel's room where she was still in bed. By about 11 a.m. the rest of the household began to worry about Angel because she usually rose between 8 and 9 a.m. The handle of the door was tried and it was found to be locked from the inside. With no response from within, the door to her room was forced open and Angel was found lying dead on the bed.

The police and a doctor were immediately sent for. The doctor observed that Angel was naked and her hair was dishevelled. Examining her body he discovered that her mouth, face, breasts and hands were covered with nitric acid. As the doctor and police searched for a bottle of poison, Lipski was found lying in his shirtsleeves on his back, under the bed. Lipski was unconscious but upon the doctor giving him a smart slap on the face, he opened his eyes. The police

Newgate Prison.
(Courtesy of Bishopsgate Institute)

took Lipski towards the window where it was observed that his lips were stained with nitric acid.

The police concluded from such a scene that Lipski must have committed the murder and then had tried to kill himself. Lipski, however, professed his innocence saying that two workmen had committed the murder and then they had tried to kill him. He further claimed that it was his two employees, Schmuss and Rosenbloom, who had committed the terrible deed.

Lipski's two-day trial took place on 29 and 30 July 1887 at the Old Bailey. Lipski was poorly defended and it took the jury just eight minutes to deliberate and conclude that he was guilty. The judge for the case was one of England's most renowned magistrates: James Fitzjames Stephen. However, Stephen was concerned about Lipski's poor defence. He was also troubled by his own unfair address to the jury which, suggesting that the motive was lust, had ruled out the possibility that more than one person had been present at the scene of the crime.

Despite the fact that the door was locked from the inside and Lipski seemed the obvious candidate for Angel's murder, there was real doubt about Lipski's guilt. The trial was tarnished by institutionalised anti-Semitism and William Thomas Stead, the editor of the *Pall Mall Gazette*, launched a press campaign to reprieve Lipski. It is said that even Queen Victoria was troubled by the prospect of Lipski being hanged solely on the evidence presented in court. The date 15 August was set for execution but it was postponed for a week while Home

ISRAEL LIPSKI AND JACK THE RIPPER

On 30 September 1888, Israel Schwartz reported witnessing a woman being assaulted on Berner Street. An unknown man shouted out 'Lipski' to either Schwartz, who was a man of Jewish appearance, or to another man and Schwartz fled. Later, the woman was identified as Elizabeth Stride who is thought to have been murdered by Jack the Ripper. This murder was only one street away from the site of Miriam Angel's murder. When the police originally investigated Stride's murder they looked at whether there was someone in the neighbourhood by the name of Lipski. There were several people named Lipski but the police eventually decided that the term had been used as an ethnic slur against Jews.

Secretary Henry Matthews and Judge Stephen met to consider the reprieve. Matthews was personally opposed to capital punishment but appears to have been apathetic to Lipski's plight. On the night before Lipski was due to hang, Lipski confessed to one of England's best-known rabbis, Simeon Singer. Lipski claimed that his motive was robbery rather than the prosecutions' claim of rape. The following morning Singer authorised the public release of the confession and on 22 August 1887 Lipski was hanged in the yard at Newgate Prison. When the black flag was raised to confirm Lipski's death the gathered crowd of over 5,000 people let out three loud cheers.

It is said that Lipski may have confessed to a murder that he did not commit in order to escape a lifetime in prison. Rabbi Singer may well have released the confession by Lipski to end the controversy surrounding the trial and thus preventing even greater problems for the Jewish community, as the case was to ignite anti-Semitic feeling in England.

As to whether Lipski actually committed the Whitechapel murder, this still remains a mystery!

AD 1888

THE WHITECHAPEL MURDERS

IN THE AUTUMN of 1888 perhaps the most famous story set in the East End began to unfold. For three months the people of Whitechapel lived in fear of Jack the Ripper, a murderer who savagely mutilated the bodies of his victims after he had cut their throat.

Whitechapel in this period was an area riddled with dark passages and courts lined with the cheapest and dirtiest of lodging houses. The inhabitants in parts were such unsavoury characters that the police did not dare to patrol alone. If they tried to make an arrest they were liable to be set upon by the crook's associates.

Perhaps Jack the Ripper was a resident here or perhaps he chose this area on purpose. Either way, in each of the five authenticated cases his victim was a prostitute of the very lowest class.

Jack the Ripper's first victim was Mary Ann Nicholls. She was discovered in Bucks Row at 3.20 a.m. on Friday, 31 August. Her throat was cut practically from ear to ear. Barely five minutes before her discovery a policeman had passed by that way and yet neither he, nor the two men who made the grisly discovery shortly afterward, saw or heard anything of the murderer.

The second victim, Annie Chapman, known as 'Dark Annie', was found in the backyard of No. 29 Hanbury Street at about daybreak on Saturday, 8 September. This was a far more gruesome murder than the first, as Dark Annie's body had been disembowelled. Death had occurred, as in the first case, by the throat being cut. Some experts said that the murderer must have had a certain degree of medical skill to carry out such mutilation

The police being mocked about the Whitechapel murders. (THP)

of the body. Once again, nobody saw or heard anything during the crime, even though the backyard was only yards from a number of people sleeping at the time. Fear amongst the local community grew and suspicions, theories and criticism of the police began to circulate.

On Sunday, 30 September, confusion reigned after the Ripper struck twice in one night. The two murders were discovered within an hour of each other and in both cases the crime had only just been committed. The first victim to be discovered was Elizabeth Stride, a 45-year-old widow who was known as 'Long Liz'. The body was found by Louis Diemschutz when he returned to his yard behind No. 40 Berner Street with his pony and cart at 1 a.m. Long Liz had had her throat cut and medical evidence suggested that she had died within the last quarter of an hour. Investigators believed that the Ripper may have been disturbed during this crime as the body had not been mutilated.

In the corner of Mitre Square, just inside the city of London, Catherine Eddowes was found a mere forty-five minutes later. Eddowes, who was 43 years old, had been murdered and mutilated. This murder was probably the most daring committed so far as Mitre Square was patrolled every fifteen minutes by the police. It was reported that at 1.30 a.m. all was quiet and the square was empty. At 1.45 a.m. the patrolling officers found Eddowes extensively mutilated in a manner that must have taken some time. Poor Eddowes had been arrested the previous night for drunkenness and had only been released from custody at 1 a.m.

The Ripper's fifth victim was Mary Jane Kelly, a pretty young woman of only 25 years of age, who was known as 'Black Mary'. Like the Ripper's previous victims she was practically penniless and addicted to drink. She was discovered on Friday, 9 November, just after 10.45 a.m. by the rent collector calling at her lodgings, No. 13 Millers Court, which was off Dorset Street. Black Mary was the only Ripper victim to be murdered indoors. Therefore her murderer presumably had more privacy and time to deal with her body in his own horrible way. As before, 'Black Mary's' throat was cut but her body was mutilated far more brutally and extensively than any other victim.

Some people believed that the Ripper himself was so horrified by the scene he had created at Millers Court that he committed suicide by drowning himself in the Thames. Others believed that he moved his activities away from London, but nobody knows for sure. To this day the identity of the Ripper is still unknown.

The only positive outcome of these appalling events was that the public's attention was drawn to the squalor and terrible conditions of the East End and steps were taken to improve conditions in the area. Bizarrely it has been suggested by some that the Ripper might have been a social reformer with this end in mind. A range of other motives and guises for the Ripper's attacks (some plausible and some less so) have been suggested over the years. Some say he was a sadist, a motiveless madman or a professional assassin hired by the Russian anarchists to discredit the British police, while others suggest that he was in fact a woman. Whoever the Ripper was, the murders that were committed have become legends in crime.

AD 1910–1911

THE HOUNDSDITCH MURDERS AND THE SIEGE OF SIDNEY STREET

T**HE EAST END** at the beginning of the twentieth century was a violent place where there was an indiscriminate use of firearms by local anarchists.

The drama began with the Tottenham Outrage, an attempted robbery that resulted in the killing of two people when the would-be robbers fired indiscriminately in the streets.

On Saturday, 23 January 1909, Paul Hefeld and Jacob Lepidus waited outside the Schnurmann rubber factory gates, Chestnut Road, Tottenham, with guns in their pockets, for the factory car to return from the London and South West Bank in Hackney with the week's wages, about £80, as it did every Saturday morning at 10.30 a.m. Arriving with the wages, Albert Keyworth got out of the car and was walking across the pavement to the factory yard when Lepidus attacked him. The two men struggled over the wages bag and then Hefeld fired at Keyworth several times in rapid succession. At this point a passer-by, George

Smith, tackled Lepidus and Keyworth seized this opportunity to stagger towards a policeman who was less than 40yds away. Hefeld fired at Smith but missed, so he grabbed him by the throat and rolled him over, seizing the wages bag. Hefeld fired once more and then the pair of thieves ran down Chestnut Road with the policeman close on their heels.

Two police constables, Tyler and Newman, were in the factory car and Lepidus and Hefeld fired at the car but ended up killing a boy, Ralph Joscelyne, in the street. They ran across the marshes to Salisbury Hall Farm and on to Chingford Road where they stopped a tram. The pursuit continued and the two men then took a milk cart after shooting the milkman. They wrecked the cart and next took a greengrocers van, which they abandoned and ran along a fence, not realising that the fence and footpath converged and that their pursuers were catching up with them. Lepidus managed to climb the fence but Hefeld, realising he was trapped, fired his gun into his own head. The bullet went in half an inch above his right eye and exploded out through his forehead on the other side. He was badly wounded but still alive. The gun was wrenched from his fingers and he was taken to the Prince of Wales Hospital covered in blood.

Lepidus ran across the railway line, through Beech Hall Estate, across Oak Hill and towards Oak Cottage. The owner's wife, Mrs Rolstone, was at home with her children and went out to the gate to watch the events. The police shouted at her to go in but when she tried she could not open the door of the lean-to. Then she saw the bloodstained face of Lepidus inside her house and screamed because her children were locked inside with him. Constables Charles Eagles and John Carter, along with Detective Constable Charles Dixon, forced their way into the house and found Lepidus in the children's room where they shot him, killing him.

The chase had lasted more than two hours and had covered 6 miles. Hefeld and Lepidus had fired over 400 rounds of ammunition, killed two and injured or wounded twenty-one, which included seven policemen. On 14 February 1909, Hefeld died from meningitis, five days after surgery to remove pieces of bone at the entrance to the wound, which were causing compression of the brain.

The Special Branch investigators suspected that a young Latvian by the name of Christian Salnish had been behind the incident and he was one of the robbers of H.S. Harris Jewellers in December 1910.

One of the Lettish gang firing his pistol at the police. (Courtesy of Bishopsgate Institute)

In December 1910, the Houndsditch Murders occurred. Christian Salnish and a group of exiled Russian revolutionaries known as 'Liesma' (Latvian for 'flame') planned to rob H.S. Harris Jewellers on Saturday, 16 December, as the shop would be shut due to the owners being Jewish. The robbers intended to tunnel through from the back of a neighbouring property. Mr Weil, who lived in the flat next door, over his fancy-goods business, returned from his evening out at about 10 p.m. to find his sister and their maidservant agitated by the unusual noises coming from downstairs at the back of the shop. Mr Weil went out on to the street to find a young constable, Walter Piper, and together they listened to the curious noise. Both agreed it sounded like drilling, sawing and the breaking away of brickwork. Piper found two more constables from adjoining beats, Walter Choate and Ernest Woodhams. He also met the duty sergeant, Robert Bentley, and two plain-clothed constables, James Martin and Arthur Strongman.

Strongman went back to the station to get the night duty inspector to telephone Harris and ask him to come and meet them at his shop.

Back outside the shop, the assembled policemen were also joined by Constable Smoothey, Sergeant Bryant and Sergeant Tucker. As they forced their way through the door, a man was holding a pistol, which he fired as he advanced towards them. Behind him on the stairs was another man who also began shooting. One of the shots fired from the stairs went straight through the rim of Bentley's helmet, across his face and out through the shutter behind him. Bryant was also shot in the arm and slightly wounded in the chest. Constable Woodhams' leg buckled beneath him as a bullet shattered his thighbone and he fell unconscious to the ground, and Tucker staggered as he was shot twice, once in the hip and once in the heart, which killed him. Choate, a large muscular man, was shot five times in total, the last two bullets being fired into his back. As he fell he dragged one of the assailants, whose name was George Gardstein, with him and a shot hit Gardstein in the back. Choate was kicked and punched in the face to make him release his grip on Gardstein, who was seized by two of the group and dragged away, but he was already a dying man.

Gardstein was taken back to his lodgings and two women associated with the group – Sara Rose Trassjonsky and Luba Milstein – were sent to tend to him and burn any evidence. Upon seeing Gardstein's wounds, the two women went to a local doctor's house for assistance. Gardstein said that a friend had shot him by accident but refused to go to the hospital. The following day Gardstein died and the doctor had to call the police. Trassjonsky stayed with the body until the police arrived and hurriedly burnt a number of papers.

On Wednesday, 21 December, Trassjonsky and Milstein were taken to Bishopsgate Street police station on charges of being an accessory to the murders of the three policemen; harbouring and assisting Gardstein; assisting the other men unknown; and conspiring with Gardstein and others unknown to break and enter Harris' shop with the intent to commit a felony.

The funerals of the murdered officers, Choate, Tucker and Bentley, took place on 22 December. The nation mourned the loss of these three policemen and was shocked that the anarchists of Europe appeared to be invading England. On Christmas Eve morning, three men, Fedoroff, Peters and Duboff, were charged with being connected with Gardstein, and others not in custody, in the murder of the three policemen; they were also charged with conspiring with Trassjonsky, Milstein, Gardstein and others to rob Harris' shop. A reward of £500 was offered for the capture of further suspects, including Fritz Svaars and 'Peter the Painter'.

On the morning of 3 January 1911 the Siege of Sidney Street began. The police converged on No. 100 Sidney Street, where they had discovered that the two remaining members of the gang were located. The occupants of the adjacent buildings were quickly evacuated and soon there were around 200 policemen at the scene, including a detachment of the 1st Scots Guards from the Tower. The policemen took up their positions in a number of vantage points and waited to see what would happen next.

Winston Churchill, who was Home Secretary at the time, went to Sidney Street to watch the events unfold. Crowds flocked into Mile End Road from the city, all bound for Sidney Street, and were kept at a distance by members of the police. A brick was thrown at one of the windows and suddenly shots rang out between the two desperate criminals and the police. A policeman, Sergeant Leeson, was wounded and the remaining inhabitants of Sidney Street

could only watch as hundreds of bullets flew in all directions as the police and members of the army returned the fire of the two gang members.

At around 1 p.m. a fire started in No. 100 Sidney Street. A reporter on the roof of the Rising Sun pub could see a gas jet burning steadily in the first-floor room of the building and it is possible that the two men within had deliberately started the fire before attempting to escape. However, they remained trapped in the house and eventually fire engulfed the entire building. The relentless barrage of fire from both sides had stopped and

The army ready to fire! (Courtesy of Bishopsgate Institute)

fire engines arrived at the scene. A strong stream of water was aimed at the blazing ruins of the house and by 2.20 p.m. the firefighters entered the building.

The two men were found, their bodies completely unrecognisable. The first body found was that of Fritz Svaars. His remains were placed in a coffin and taken to the Horseferry Branch Road Mortuary. It took another five hours before Josef Sokoloff's body was found as it had been covered by debris. It was believed that one of the men, during the gunfire, had leaned too far out of the window and instantly became the target for concentrated fire. It seems likely from the subsequent evidence that he had been killed at the time by a bullet through the brain.

On 6 January 1911 at Stepney's Coroners Court the jury decided that Josef's death had been caused by a wound inflicted by an unknown soldier and thus justifiable homicide. From the position of the entrance and exit wounds in the head there was little

No. 100 Sidney Street on fire!
(Courtesy of Bishopsgate Institute)

doubt that he had been shot and had not committed suicide. Fritz was found by the doorway of the same room in which Josef had been found, and it was presumed that he had died where he was found from suffocation.

AD 1917

AIR RAID ON UPPER NORTH STREET SCHOOL

DURING THE FIRST World War, the East End of London was one of the most targeted places. On Wednesday, 13 June 1917, fourteen Gotha aeroplanes, carrying an average load of ten bombs each, attacked London with unprecedented violence. The Zeppelin raids at night had been terrifying enough but this new daylight raid was even worse because the streets, houses and shops were bustling with people going about their daily lives. The death and mutilation caused by this raid was

Damage at Upper North Street School. (Courtesy of Tower Hamlets Local History Library and Archives)

A man digging through the rubble at Upper North Street School.
(Courtesy of Tower Hamlets Local History Library and Archives)

considerable. Liverpool Street station was hit and a train there was destroyed causing thirteen fatalities and many injuries. It was a tragic loss of life that could have been avoided had the city police warned the station authorities of the raid and the people in the area had been evacuated. In the East End 104 people were killed, 154 seriously injured and 269 slightly injured.

The gravest incident that day was the damage done to Upper North Street School, Poplar. The top floor of the school was the girls' class, the middle floor was the boys' class and on the ground floor was the infant class of about fifty students. At the sound of an air raid the children were told to stand against the walls, so that anything that fell through the middle of the room would not hurt them. The 50kg (110lb) bomb penetrated the roof of the school proceeding through the girls' class, down through the boys' classroom and exploded in the infant class. In all eighteen students were killed, sixteen of which were from the infants' class. The two teachers, Mrs Midleton and Miss Watkins, who were uninjured themselves, worked heroically to ensure that the remainder of the infants' class got out of the building. Then they helped others rescue bodies from the rubble. The children who had been killed were quickly removed to the mortuary and nurses and surgeons at the local hospitals cared for those who were injured.

The funeral for the schoolchildren of Upper North Street School.
(Courtesy of Tower Hamlets Local History Library and Archives)

The school was situated in close proximity to East India Dock Road and the hit upon the school would appear to have been the result of a rather poor aim, directed either at the docks themselves or at the very busy thoroughfare with all its heavy morning traffic. The leader of the German raiders that day, Hauptmann Brandenburg, thought that he had attacked a railway station, the docks and Tower Bridge.

Will Crooks, the local MP, expressed his grave sorrow for all those affected by the bombing.

The funeral held for these infants, about a week later, was one of the biggest funerals in London. The Bishop

> The death of so many schoolchildren, in this one incident, became one of the main reasons for the carefully planned evacuation of children during the Second World War.

of London, Arthur Foley Winnington-Ingram, and the Bishop of Stepney, Henry Luke Paget, took the service. Fifteen of the children were buried in one grave at the East London Cemetery. The three remaining children had private graves.

AD 1936

THE BATTLE OF CABLE STREET

EAST ENDERS WILL always remember Sunday, 4 October 1936, as it was the day of the Battle of Cable Street, a battle between Fascists and non-Fascists. The British Union of Fascists (BUF), led by Oswald Mosley, marched into Cable Street and were met by anti-Fascists, including Jewish, Socialist, Anarchist, Irish and Communist groups.

On 26 September 1936, Mosley had announced that he and his party members intended to march from Tower Hill through Cable Street and on into the predominantly Jewish area of Stepney. Such news was greeted with alarm and dismay. The planned march was viewed as a calculated act of anti-Semitic provocation. The Jewish People's Council called for the march

The barricades on Cable Street. (Courtesy of Bishopsgate Institute)

to be banned and organised a petition that was signed by 100,000 people. The Communist Party in the local district claimed that Mosley was provoking disorder and racial strife in the East End. However, the government's view was that a ban on the march would appear undemocratic and therefore Phil Piratin, the leader of the Communist Party, decided that he would lead an opposing march.

On the morning of the battle it was a bright autumnal day. From the narrow courts, alleyways and main thoroughfares came the sound of marching feet. Anti-Fascists were gathering, including many who had travelled to the area in support of the cause, and banners filled the scene with the words 'They Shall Not Pass' displayed in a variety of colours, but predominantly red. A number of chants filled the air, including 'Bar the road to fascism!' Loudspeaker vans were used up and down the streets, booming out the message for everyone to rally to the defence line at Cable Street and Gardiners Corner. Thousands of ordinary people who had never taken part in political activity before were out on the streets.

The anti-Fascist groups built barricades formed of bricks, ladders, planks of wood and anything that they could find to block the road. The first of these barricades was at Leman Street and more were erected at the junction of Christian Street.

It was estimated that 100,000 anti-Fascist protestors greeted the Fascists while 6,000 police officers tried to clear the crowds in order to allow the 2–3,000 Fascist marchers to proceed with their demonstration. The police aimed to keep Leman Street clear;

however, the whole of Gardiners Corner was blocked by a tram that had been left standing by its anti-Fascist driver and the police, unable to move this roadblock, were forced to turn their attention elsewhere. Another very effective blockade was just past Back Church Lane where the Communist Party had overturned a builder's lorry across the road where the Fascists were marching in from the Leman Street end. Time and time again the police charged the barricades in an attempt to clear the way for Mosley, but the defenders were too numerous and determined.

When the Blackshirts reached Cable Street they found the East Enders waiting for them. The protestors attacked with sticks, rocks, chair legs and anything else they could improvise as a weapon. Rubbish, rotten vegetables and worse were thrown at the police and marbles or fireworks were used to scare the police officers' horses. Paving stones were pulled up from the street and used as missiles or to strengthen barricades and a number of shop windows were broken during the commotion.

After a series of run-in battles, Mosley finally agreed to abandon the march in order to prevent bloodshed. The BUF marchers were sent off towards Hyde Park to disperse but the anti-Fascists continued to riot with the police, with many arrests occurring. There were also many injuries and in the aftermath of the event, people covered in blood or hastily bandaged up walked the streets. Debris was everywhere and it took some time for the street to return to normal. The battle continued to be a talking point and people would ask each other where they were

The Battle of Cable Street. (Courtesy of Bishopsgate Institute)

on 4 October. The anti-Fascists saw the Fascist abandonment of the march as a great victory for their movement, but the Jewish population were greatly unnerved and feared that something like this could happen again.

In the aftermath of the battle, severe restrictions were placed on marches. The Council of Citizens of East London led a successful campaign for the prohibition of political uniforms to be worn, which passed into law in the Public Orders Act.

By the 1980s a permanent reminder had been commissioned to mark the 50th anniversary of the Battle of Cable Street and a mural depicting the battle was painted on the west wall of St George's Town Hall, Cable Street. Prior to the completion of the mural, Fascists climbed the scaffolding and defaced the

> Phil Piratin's role in leading the non-Fascists was recognised locally. The following year he became the first Communist to be elected to the Stepney Borough Council. In 1945 Piratin was voted a Communist MP for Mile End.

mural, writing on it, 'British Nationalism not Communism – Rights for Whites Stop the Race War' in 6ft-high letters and effectively destroyed the bottom two-thirds of the artwork. The mural has been vandalised on a number of occasions by Fascist movements. By the 1990s a special varnish was applied to the mural so that future attacks could be cleaned off easily.

AD 1943

BETHNAL GREEN
SHELTER DISASTER

THE BETHNAL GREEN Shelter Disaster was one of the worst tragedies of the Second World War in the East End.

In the 1930s work had begun to extend the Central line eastwards, and by the outbreak of war, the tunnels were largely completed although the railway line had not yet been laid. In 1940, with the onset of the Blitz, the facilities at Bethnal Green underground station were requisitioned and administrated by the local authority, under the supervision of the London Civil Defence. As one of the few deep-level stations in the East End, Bethnal

The entrance to Bethnal Green Tube Station.
(Courtesy of Tower Hamlets Local History Library and Archives)

Green underground station was an obvious choice as a public bomb shelter. The shelter was situated in a densely populated urban area and it contained some 5,000 bunks. During some of the heaviest raids it was reported to have sheltered some 7,000 people. By October 1940, heavy raids were pouring down over London and thousands of people took shelter in the tunnels, often staying overnight. However, by 1941, as the air raids were concentrated away from London, the usage of the shelter dwindled.

On 1 March 1943 there had been a heavy bombing raid on Berlin, so people were expecting a retaliatory strike any day. By 3 March, they thought that day had arrived when the Civil Defence air-raid siren sounded at 8.17 p.m. When the siren sounded approximately 500 people were already safely in the underground station, hundreds more would join them in anticipation of a heavy raid. The Germans had switched bombing tactics from slow, heavy aircraft to lighter, faster bombers; thus giving people less time to reach shelter. The people of Bethnal Green knew this and when they heard the sirens they poured out of the cinemas or got off the passing buses and headed towards the station.

Within the first ten minutes of the sirens sounding, some 1,500 people had passed safely into the shelter, without undue haste or sign of panic. Due to the blackouts there was only a 25-watt light bulb to guide people from the street into the shelter. At the bottom of the steps was a landing and from here people turned right and descended

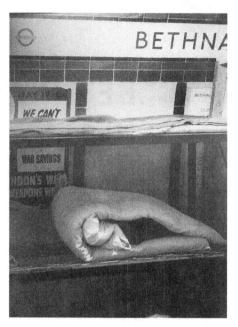

The 'Bundle Shop'. (Courtesy of Tower Hamlets Local History Library and Archives)

another set of steps to the ticket hall. From the ticket hall there were a set of escalators that led to the platforms and safety; some 80ft below ground. It had also been raining on the day of the raid, so the steps down to the shelter were wet and no doubt slippery, making the descent treacherous.

For many, the nightly move to the underground station was nothing new. Families would already have their bedding stored at the 'Bundle Shop', a left luggage depot, in the underground station. As soon as the air raid sounded a member of the family would head off to get their bedding and then go down to the platform to grab a decent place.

At 8.27 p.m. there was a frightening roar as an anti-aircraft battery fired its salvo of sixty rockets. The sound of the battery was unfamiliar and peoples' apprehension now turned to panic

Handrails being fitted on the stairs. (Courtesy of Tower Hamlets Local History Library and Archives)

as they dashed to the shelter. As the crowd surged down the slippery steps a woman holding her child and bedding bundle fell near the bottom of the first staircase. Then an elderly man tripped over her and others tumbled helplessly on top of them forming a tangled and immovable mass of bodies. However, unaware of what was happening at the bottom of the staircase, people kept surging forward seeking safety in the shelter.

As mass panic ensued, rescue attempts were severely hampered. A police constable soon arrived on the scene as he escorted his pregnant wife to the shelter. In order to assess the situation, PC Thomas Penn crawled over the tangled bodies to the bottom

of the staircase. He found nearly 300 people squeezed into a tiny stairwell some 15ft by 11ft wide. PC Penn then climbed out again in order to send a message for help; after which he returned down the staircase to help pull people free. Others quickly came to help the rescue operation. Many were safely extracted but 173 people, eighty-four women, sixty-two children and twenty-seven men, were crushed or asphyxiated. Approximately sixty others were taken to hospital. The woman who originally fell reportedly survived the incident but her child did not.

The whole area was cleaned up and all evidence of the event was removed. The British Government was fearful that

The lack of deep air-raid shelters in the East End was highlighted by the Stepney Tenants Defence League (STDL) when, at 8 p.m. on the night of 14 September 1940, the Savoy Hotel shelter was taken over by East Enders. The STDL stated that they wanted the Tube stations to be opened as public shelters. Two days later Herbert Morrison, Home Secretary, announced in Parliament that Tube stations would be fitted out for the occupation of people, with refreshments being provided.

news of such an unnecessary disaster would severely damage public morale. Reporting of the disaster was delayed for thirty-six hours and even when it was released, it was heavily censored, and neither the precise location nor the number of fatalities was released. A public inquiry was demanded, but this was not to be the case. It was considered by the government that such an inquiry would give disproportionate importance to the incidence and might encourage further enemy raids. Instead a secret official report was made by Laurence Rivers Dunne, a Metropolitan magistrate, which acknowledged that the Bethnal Green Council had warned the London Civil Defence in 1941 that the staircase needed a crush barrier in order to slow down the crowds. Bethnal Green Council, however, had been told that such a barrier would be a waste of money. Herbert Morrison, the Minister of Home Security, acknowledged receipt of the inquiry and said that action was being taken to prevent further disasters happening.

The Bethnal Green Shelter Disaster is thought to have been the largest single loss of civilian life in the United Kingdom during the Second World War. It is also thought to be the greatest loss of life in a single incident on the London Underground Network.

ABOUT THE AUTHOR

DR SAMANTHA L. BIRD has spent over a decade researching the history of the East End of London and collecting some of the gruesome and violent stories that appear in *Bloody British History: East End*. She has a PhD based on her East End research, which specialised in Stepney Borough. She is also author of two publications on the East End: *Stepney: Profile of a London Borough from the Outbreak of the First World War to the Festival of Britain 1914–1951*, the first authoritative, dedicated history of this area of London during the twentieth century, and *Stepney Then & Now*, published by The History Press.

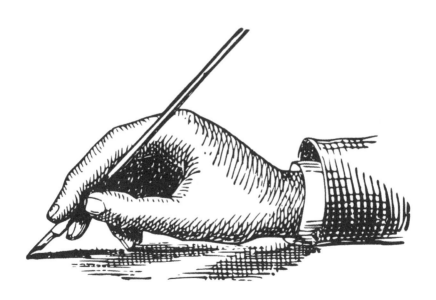

BIBLIOGRAPHY

Books

Bailey, Brian, *The Resurrection Men: A History of the Trade in Corpses* (London: Macdonald, 1991)

Bailey, James Blake, *The Diary of a Resurrectionist 1811–1812* (London: Swan Sonnenschein & Co., 1896)

Ball, James Moores, *The Sack-'em-up Men: An Account of the Rise and Fall of the Modern Resurrectionists* (London: Oliver & Boyd, 1928)

Bird, Samantha L., *Stepney: Profile of a London Borough from the Outbreak of the First World War to the Festival of Britain, 1914–1951* (Cambridge Scholars Publishing, 2011)

Bleackley, Horace, *Jack Sheppard* (William Hodge & Co., 1933)

Bleackley, Horace, *The Hangmen of England* (London: Chapman and Hall, 1929)

Buffery, J., *London Witchcraft* (James Pike Ltd, 1977)

Darby, Madge, *Captain Bligh in Wapping* (History of Wapping Trust, 1990)

Darby, Madge, *Piety and Piracy: The History of Wapping and St Katherine's* (History of Wapping Trust, 2011)

Ewen, C. L'Estrange (ed.), *Witch Hunting and Witch Trials* (Kessinger Publishing, 2010)

Fagan, Hymie, *Nine Days that Shook England* (Victor Gollancz, 1938)

Fido, Martin, *Bodysnatchers: A History of the Resurrectionists 1742–1832* (Weidenfeld & Nicolson Ltd, 1988)

Finch, Harold, *Tower Hamlets Connection: A Biographical Guide* (Tower Hamlets, 1996)

Grainger, Ian, Duncan Hawkins, Lynne Cowal and Richard Mikulski (eds), *The Black Death Cemetery, East Smithfield, London* (Museum of London Archaeology Service, 2008)

Jones, Lincoln S., *Colonel Thomas Rainsborough: Wapping's Most Famous Soldier* (History of Wapping Trust, 1991)

Kerrigan, Colm, *A History of Tower Hamlets* (Tower Hamlets, 1982)

Lee, Ernest C., *A Short History of the Parish Church of Whitechapel* (called in olden times St Mary Matfelon) (School-Press, 1887)

Locks, Walter A. (ed.), *East London Antiquities: Some Records of East London in the Days of Old, Its History, Legends, Folk-lore and Topography* (East London Advertiser, 1902)

Maitland, William, *A History of London* (Samuel Richardson, 1739)

Richardson, John, *The Annals of London: A Year-by-Year Record of a Thousand Years of History* (University of California Press, 2000)

Robinson, *The Witch of Wapping* (W.R., 1843)

Sidney, Philip, *The Headsman of Whitehall* (Kessinger Publishing, 1905)

Stepney Borough Council, *The Metropolitan Borough of Stepney, Official Guide* (Burrow, 1952)

Thomson, Richard, *Legends of London and Chronicles of the Olden Times* (J. Pattie, 1839)

Weinreb, Ben, Christopher Hibbert, John Keay and Julia Keay, *London Encyclopedia* (Macmillan, 2008)

Wilson, Henry, *The Book of Wonderful Characters: Memoirs and Anecdotes of Remarkable and Eccentric Persons in all Ages and Countries* (J. Robins & Co. Albion Press, 1821)

Wyld, Peter, *Stepney Story: A Thousand Years of St Dunstan's* (The Saint Catherine Press, 1952)

ARCHIVES

Bishopsgate Institute
  London Collection
  Howell Collection
Tower Hamlets Local History Library
  and Archives

NEWSPAPERS AND MAGAZINES

East End News
East London Advertiser
Illustrated London News
The Gentleman's Magazine

ONLINE SOURCES

British History Online:
  www.british-history.ac.uk
Idea Stores:
  www.ideastore.co.uk/local-history-online-exhibitions-upper-north-street-school-air-raid-june-1917
Lubin:
  www.lubin.co.uk/?p=335
Mail Online for the Bethnal Green Tube tragedy:
  www.dailymail.co.uk/news/article-521490
Oxford Dictionary of National Biography
  www.oxforddnb.com
Spitalfields Life
  www.spitalfieldslife.com
Victorian London
  www.victorianlondon.org/crime/harrietlane.htm
WW2 People's War
  www.bbc.co.uk/history/ww2peopleswar/stories/09/a795909.shtml

Lightning Source UK Ltd.
Milton Keynes UK
UKOW06f2134190615

253810UK00002B/5/P